Buffalo Bill
Myth & Reality

Show poster of Cody. Cody's posters were the best of the era, and according to contemporaries Cody was the handsomest man of the period. Courtesy of the Buffalo Bill Historical Center, Cody, Wyoming.

Buffalo Bill Myth & Reality

by Eric V. Sorg

Ancient City Press ⟿ Santa Fe, New Mexico

Cover art and design by Margaret Donharl
Book design and typesetting by Kathleen Sparkes, White Hart Designs

Sorg, Eric V.
  Buffalo Bill: Myth and Reality / Eric V. Sorg
        p.   cm.
  Includes Bibliographical references (p.   )
  ISBN 1–58096–002–2 (cloth: alk. paper). —
  ISBN 1–58096–003–0 (paper: alk. paper)
        1. Buffalo Bill, 1846–1917. 2. Pioneers—West (U.S.)—Biography.
  3. Entertainers—United States—Biography. 4. Buffalo Bill's Wild West
  Show— History. 5. West (U.S.)—Biography I. Title
  F594.S69   1998
  978'.02'092—dc21
  [B]   98-2629
                                                                  CIP

10   9   8   7   6   5   4   3   2   1

Contents

Dedication

I dedicate this work and every essay I write to Mom, Pop, and Porky, who were friends when I needed friendship most and others turned away.

Acknowledgments

I HAVE HAD THE JOY OF RESEARCHING WILLIAM CODY AND HIS colleagues in many libraries, museums, and historical societies throughout the country. If I neglected to mention any in the following list, I apologize for the oversight. Included are: the American Heritage Center, Laramie, Wyoming; the Bieneke Library, New Haven, Connecticut; the Buffalo Bill Historical Center, Cody, Wyoming; the Carbon County Clerk's Office, Rawlins, Wyoming; the Circus World Museum, Baraboo, Wisconsin; the Denver Public Library, Denver, Colorado; the Fillmore County Clerk's Office, Preston, Minnesota; the Grand Encampment Museum, Encampment, Wyoming; the Kansas State Historical Society, Topeka, Kansas; the La Crosse County Clerk's Office, La Crosse, Wisconsin; the La Crosse Historical Society, La Crosse, Wisconsin; the Lanesboro Historical Society, Lanesboro, Minnesota; the Library of Congress, Washington, D.C.; the Merrick County Clerk's Office, Central City, Nebraska; the Minnesota Historical Society, St. Paul, Minnesota; the Murphy Special Collections, University of Wisconsin, La Crosse, Wisconsin; the National Archives, Washington, D.C.; the National Museum of American History, Washington, D.C.; the National Anthropological Archives, Washington, D.C.; the Nebraska State Historical Society, Lincoln, Nebraska; the Omaha Historical Society, Omaha, Nebraska; the Park County Historical Society, Cody, Wyoming; the Scout's Rest Museum, North Platte, Nebraska; the University of Louisville, Louisville, Kentucky; the Wisconsin State Historical Society, Madison, Wisconsin; and the Wyoming State Archives, Cheyenne, Wyoming.

I am also grateful to Christina Stopka, Elizabeth Holmes, and Thomas Morrison. My thesis committee was composed of Eric Sandeen, Sonny Bahs, and Paul Fees. Special thanks to

Paul Fees, the senior curator for the Buffalo Bill Historical Center and leading authority on William Cody, who was tolerant of my eccentric ways and was especially important in guiding my understanding of William Cody of the "Indian wars."

Dime novel cover. Both as authors and as subjects William Cody and Frank Powell knew that dime novels were good business. Courtesy of the Sorg Collection.

Introduction

WILLIAM F. CODY'S LIFE WAS SHAPED LIKE A CLASSICAL tragedy etched across the western prairies. Although the popular media has sometimes portrayed Cody as a racist who was very adept at killing buffalo and through self-aggrandizement in show business made a fortune that he squandered, my research about Cody indicates the opposite is true—that Cody was an enlightened egalitarian who lived a classically tragic life. A charming and humorous man, Cody was a respected frontiersman who saw the opportunity to turn his solid Plains credentials into a secure future for his family and investment capital for himself in the fanciful world of theatrics. However, while in show business Cody became trapped by his guileless nature and his desire to contribute to the advancement of society. Cody's last few years were his most tragic and most heroic. To quote Gene Fowler, "He lived with the world at his feet and died with it on his shoulders."[1]

For a person who has been called a charlatan and a braggart, Cody was a man of remarkable accomplishments and modesty. While serving with the army as a civilian scout from September 1868 through November 1872, Cody was credited with fourteen expeditions against Indians. Although the average soldier was in one battle during a five-year period, Cody fought in fifteen. Often mentioned in reports for his daring and bravery, he was awarded the Congressional Medal of Honor. Frequently, when nobody else dared, Cody volunteered to deliver messages between military columns through hostile territory at great personal risk. No other scout who served with the military could boast of accomplishments close to these. Yet this man who was called a braggart played these actions down in his 1879 autobiography, turning several of them into jokes, with himself as the clown.

The popular media and Cody himself have so twisted the facts of his life throughout the years that for the majority of the

Daniel Boone was the first American frontier hero to capture the public's imagination. Courtesy of the Sorg Collection.

American public the historic Cody and the culture he presented to 70 million people have been lost. The major reason for the modern warped viewpoint of Cody is that he was so successful in capitalizing on his solid accomplishments.

More dime novels were written about "Buffalo Bill" than any other western character, and *Buffalo Bill's Wild West* was a successful business venture for decades; millions of people saw it worldwide. Cody insisted on authenticity in his show but highlighted the unusual rather than focusing on the mundane. Thus, Indians wore long flowing headdresses, cowboys inevitably arrived in the nick of time, and the audience always left with a feeling of awe. Among others, Mark Twain, Libby Custer, and General Phillip Sheridan wrote of the realistic depiction of the West as presented by Cody.

Cody and the West were the end products of a long legacy of romantic thought about the frontier, a frontier that ceased to exist during his lifetime. With the cynicism of the modern era, the public has sometimes found it easier to scoff at Cody's life than to be engaged by the heroic world he personified.

To find the truth about Cody, I have researched primary material scattered in museums, libraries, and other locations around the country, including countless rolls of microfilm and purported historic graffiti. Histories written during Cody's lifetime and shortly after his death are of little value in determining the truth about Cody's life since many writers contemporary with Cody, such as James Buel, created fabrications about Buffalo Bill, or, like Luther North, had axes to grind.[2] Don Russell is the most often cited authority on Cody, and his 1960 *The Lives and Legends of Buffalo Bill* is my principal source for information about Cody's early life. Russell used primary material, interviewed Cody's friends such as General Charles King, and made educated deductions from the available material when warranted. However, because new information has surfaced since Russell wrote his biography, some of Russell's statements need to be revised.[3]

During my research, it rapidly became clear to me, as it has for many interviewers and contemporary acquaintances, that there were actually two Codys. According to Cody's business partner, Nate Salsbury, "There were two of them.... One the true Cody as he has always been from his birth, and the other... a commercial proposition...."[4] The two parts of this book, *Buffalo Bill: Myth and Reality*, reflect this observation. Part 1 discusses the myth of Buffalo Bill, how it was created, and its commercial success. Part 2 focuses on the man William F. Cody and the reality of his life.

Part 1
The Myth of Buffalo Bill

The striking Cody standing in profile dressed like Daniel Boone. The similarity between the clothing of Cody and Daniel Boone was probably not coincidental. Courtesy of the Buffalo Bill Historical Center, Cody, Wyoming.

WHEN WILLIAM CODY MADE HIS STAGE DEBUT IN 1872 as Buffalo Bill, the American West was rapidly becoming civilized: the Civil War had ended only seven years before; in Germany a process for tanning buffalo hides had just been perfected, supporting the industrial revolution with tough leather belts; the wholesale slaughter of the Plains Indians' food supply had been encouraged by the military to control the first Americans; and four years later General George Armstrong Custer's famous "Custer luck" would run out in Montana. Reconstruction was a failure, and the sectional strife which existed before the Civil War was still present in a muted form. Industrialization was reshaping American culture as the slow exodus from farms became a stampede to cities.

Professional groups, labor unions, and the new middle class were in their infancy. In 1893, at Chicago's Columbian Exposition, America showed its adolescent muscle, while nearby Frederick Jackson Turner presented his thesis "The Frontier in American History," in which he suggested that the American West was a place of "perennial rebirth" for the American people. He also stated that the western frontier was now closed.[1]

Daniel Boone, Kit Carson, and Jim Bridger told fantastic stories of the sights they had seen in their travels, sights which sounded far-fetched and mythic to the comfortable eastern public. But by 1872 the West was rapidly becoming civilized, and the myth of the rugged western frontiersman was about to enter a new realm as William Cody, or Buffalo Bill, started to capitalize on the Leatherstocking myth and elevate it to new heights.

Origins of the Buffalo Bill Myth

MYTHS ARE GENERALLY ABOUT GODS AND HEROIC, moral men who were larger than life. Every culture has myth, which Henry Nash Smith defines as "an intellectual construction that fuses concept and emotion into image. The myths... have the further characteristic of being collective representations rather than the work of a single mind."[2]

The mythology surrounding William Cody has its roots in many factual aspects of his life. However, early folklore, newspaper articles, dime novels, plays, histories, and most importantly *Buffalo Bill's Wild West* all served to confuse the real life of William Cody with the mythic image of Buffalo Bill. Cody was the genuine article who became a "personality" because of solid honorable deeds in a dirty, sordid war. He used his fame to make money and help fulfill his dream of a civilized West. Because the Buffalo Bill persona was inflated for commercial gains, the reality of William Cody's life was, for the general public, lost.

In his article "The 'Wild West,'" Richard Slotkin states that Cody was aware of the ways in which popular and historical literature reinforced the mythic past of the American frontier, and built himself into a mythic figure; he used the "Leatherstocking/Buffalo Bill myth" to help in his commercial enterprises. Slotkin feels that this was why the 1888 *Story of the Wild West and Campfire Chats by Buffalo Bill (Hon. W. F. Cody)* was published.[3] This book is not only a reprinting of Cody's 1879 autobiography but also includes the biographies of Daniel Boone, Davy Crockett, and Kit Carson. Through this book Cody linked himself to the American frontier mythic past. Cody had a greater opportunity to capitalize on this past than his predecessors, and he utilized it to the utmost.

In order to examine the Buffalo Bill myth in detail, it is necessary to first consider some factual background information about Cody's life.

The Cody family Bible states that William Frederick Cody was born in LeClare, Iowa, on February 26, 1846, although Cody often gave the year of his birth as 1845—one of the many examples of Cody's bad memory for dates. His father, Isaac, got "gold fever" when Cody was four years old, and the family, which included his mother, Mary, and their children Martha, Julia, William, Eliza Alice, Laura Ellen, and Mary Hannah, headed for California. However, they only made it as far as Kansas, where the Cody family was one of the first to settle. There Isaac Cody became involved with Kansas politics, and while he was making a speech about Kansas becoming a free state instead of a slave state at Rively's Trading Post outside of Fort Leavenworth he was stabbed. The wound evidently never healed properly, and Isaac died from it two years later.

Isaac's injury and the persecution that the Cody family suffered during the border wars such as searches, seizure of property, and repeated attempts on Isaac's life, started Cody on an adventurous life before the age of ten. In many of the later biographies and histories, these adventures became fantastic stories, but Cody's sister Julia wrote a realistic account of those early years. Julia's spelling and diction are, like her brother's, poor; but what is convincing about her account, which was buried in Kansas archives for years before being published in the *Kansas Historical Quarterly*, are the human elements that give it a realistic flavor. For example, Julia recalls burning William's filthy clothes after his first trip on the

Plains, and Cody making a ride, while sick, to warn his father about an ambush; in her narrative Cody vomits all over his horse.[4] While Isaac was alive, William evidently rode on a number of occasions to save his father from assassination attempts, and most of his adventures during that time were on horseback. Unlike the accounts of Cody's sister Helen, which glorify her brother, Julia's down-to-earth family history makes these incidents believable.

When William Cody was eleven, Isaac Cody died, leaving William as the only breadwinner of the family. Because William's mother Mary was ill, Julia managed the household while William went to work for the freighting firm of Russell, Majors, and Waddell. He evidently began as a message boy and eventually worked in every position the firm could offer.

At fourteen Cody started riding a regular route on the Pony Express for Joseph Alfred Slade, and while under Slade's supervision Cody made the third longest ride, and the fastest, in the company's history. One day he galloped into his home station, Three Crossings, and found that his relief rider had been killed in a drunken row the night before. Cody did not hesitate to undertake the extra ride of eighty-five miles to Rocky Ridge and arrived there on time. He then turned back and rode the entire route back again, thus accomplishing a round-trip of 322 miles. It took him twenty-one hours and forty minutes to do it, and he went through twenty-one horses.[5]

Sometime during this period Cody also made the acquaintance of James B. Hickok (Wild Bill), and they became close friends. Hickok was nine years older than Cody and taught him the finer points of shooting and how to behave like a gentleman, something Cody was in need of since he had been a rugged, unrefined individual. For a while, Cody worked for Hickok as sort of an assistant. One time when they were done driving a mule train to Rolla, Missouri, they heard about the races scheduled in St. Louis. Hickok had just bought a fast horse named "Old Mountain," and he and Cody went to St. Louis to race the horse. Cody rode, and believing they had a sure thing, they bet everything on the race, including the horse. Unfortunately, they lost and were broke in the biggest town either one of them had ever been in. During the Civil War, Hickok secured a position as a scout; later he worked in Cody's theatrical company *Buffalo Bill's Combination* for a time.

When the Civil War broke out, Cody didn't enlist immediately because of a promise he had made to his mother to support his sisters; if he were killed, his family would be destitute. Cody did, however, scout for various military and paramilitary commands, and finally joined the regulars on February 19, 1864, after his mother died. His Civil War career was largely uneventful except that he met his future wife, Louisa Frederici.

He married "Lulu," as she was known, and tried to settle down by opening the Golden Rule Hotel near Grasshopper Falls, Kansas, the town Isaac Cody had platted. But, because Cody invited most of his friends to stay with him and generally didn't ask to be paid for his hospitality, the Codys often had financial problems.

Cody and his grading partner William Rose then founded the Kansas town of Rome. However, because they didn't give the Kansas Pacific Railroad, represented by Dr. William E. Webb, any part of the town, the railroad's routing was moved a mile north to Hays, Kansas,[6] which caused the economic decline of Rome and consequently Cody's financial ruin. Despite these facts, an article from the Ellis County Historical Society's *Homesteader* states that Rome was closed by the military because soldiers drank too much whiskey in Rome's saloons.[7]

Even though Cody lost financially in founding the town of Rome, it was his connections with the Kansas Pacific Railroad that ultimately led to the acquisition of his famous nickname and a new image. Cody and Rose, the two founders of Rome, had a grading contract for the Kansas Pacific Railroad, and during the completion of the contract Cody became better acquainted with Webb and various officers. The Goddard brothers then hired Cody in October 1867 to supply the Kansas Pacific Railroad with buffalo meat. Many of the buffalo heads taken from his kills were used to adorn station waiting rooms on the trains' routes. By the time the con-

Ned Buntline (Edward Zane Carroll Judson), Buffalo Bill Cody, Giuseppina Morlacchi, and Texas Jack Omohundro from the first of Cody's dramas, The Scouts of the Prairie. *Texas Jack and Morlacchi later married. Courtesy of the Buffalo Bill Historical Center, Cody, Wyoming.*

tract was over in May of 1868, Cody had killed 4,280 buffalo and was known as "Buffalo Bill."

On the recommendations of Hickok and Webb, Cody then became a free-lance scout for various cavalry units and came to the attention of General Phillip Sheridan in the fall of 1868 when Cody volunteered to carry important dispatches to several forts when nobody else would go. Sheridan realized the value of a scout with Cody's integrity and willingness to undertake "impossible" missions and made Cody chief of scouts for the newly formed Fifth Cavalry regiment, commanded in the field by General Eugene Carr. Scouts were not used by the military as fighters, except for Brevet Brigadier General George A. "Sandy" Forsyth's scouts famous for the Beecher's Island Battle. Instead, scouts were used to guide military columns through the wilderness and to induce them to fight; these scouts were given the accoutrements of any enemy they killed in battle. Cody's fame and popularity with the officers he scouted for was primarily the result of his willingness to undertake dangerous missions. However, Cody also fought in many battles and was awarded the Congressional Medal of Honor in 1872. The qualities that won the respect of the officers he served under were succinctly stated by General Carr in a tribute to Cody written in 1876:

> *He was very modest and unassuming. He is a natural gentleman in his manners as well as in character, and has none of the roughness of the typical frontiersman…. His eyesight is better than a good field glass; he is the best trailer I ever heard of, and also the best judge of the "lay of the country"—that is he is able to tell what kind of country is ahead, so as to know how to act. He is the perfect judge of distance, and always ready to tell correctly how many miles it is to water, or to any place, or how many miles have been marched. Mr. Cody seemed never to tire and was always ready to go, in the darkest night or the worst weather, and usually volunteered, knowing what the emergency required…. In a fight Mr. Cody is never noisy, obstreperous, or excited. In fact, I never hardly notice him in a fight, unless I happen to want him, or he has something to report, when he was always in the right place, and his information was always valuable and reliable.[8]*

In this brief sketch of Cody's career on the Great Plains, his actions do not appear to be heroic in the sense of George Pickett's or George Armstrong Custer's careers. In fact, the acclaim Cody received prior to 1887 was for his services as a scout, a Leatherstocking—acclaim given him from generals Carr, Emory, Augur, and Sheridan. Except for the heroic actions published in dime novels beginning in 1869, prior to 1887 most of this acclaim was expressed in private between military men. However, in 1887

"Arizona John" Burke, the press agent for *Buffalo Bill's Wild West*, got written letters from these and other Indian fighters to present to the British government and public as part of Cody's credentials. General Sheridan said of Cody:

> *When Bill Cody is with a command I sleep easy; he has always been successful on the trail and victorious in battle. A guide's duties are to prevent disaster and avoid the halo of glory attending a soldier's requiem. Buffalo Bill's preeminence and fame lies in the fact that he is living—for a dead scout is not worth a d__m.*[9]

It is interesting to note that many of the incidents in Cody's career on the Plains which the public saw and still sees as heroic, such as the killing of Tall Bull or Yellow Hand, are not the incidents that won Cody the enormous respect given him by the military. Also, Cody became a mythic figure not only because of his hunting or because of actions in battle but as a result of his admirable character traits. From childhood on, Cody's career was one of solid accomplishment built on the precepts of duty, loyalty, and honesty in a hostile world where one mistake could cost you your life. With such character traits guiding his actions, it was easy for Cody, or Buffalo Bill, to become a mythic character. Ironically, although Cody thrived on the Plains, the admirable character traits acquired during his life there would eventually destroy Cody in the new world that was being formed around him.

The name of "Buffalo Bill" was first brought to the attention of the eastern reading public by Edward Zane Carroll Judson, who used the pen name Ned Buntline. At the end of July 1869, he came to Fort McPherson on his way home from a temperance lecture tour in California. Shortly after he arrived, Major Brown offered to let Buntline go along on a scouting mission with Cody, and Buntline accepted.[10] While they were out scouting, Buntline asked Cody a number of questions. There is no record of what questions Buntline asked, but in the *New York Weekly* of December 23, 1869, Buntline published the first of a series of articles entitled "Buffalo

James Butler Hickok, John B. Omohundro, and William Cody, known as the Flamboyant Fraternity. All three of these authentic Plains men tried to translate their solid "western" credentials into lucrative careers as showmen: "Wild Bill" Hickok's Wild West-style entertainment flopped dismally in Buffalo, New York; "Texas Jack" Omohundro died in Leadville before the phenomenon took off; only "Buffalo Bill" Cody had what it took to succeed. Courtesy of the Buffalo Bill Historical Center, Cody, Wyoming.

Bill: The King of the Border Men."[11] Although most of the stories from this series are rehashings of Wild Bill Hickok's adventures during the Civil War with Cody's name substituted for Hickok's, through them the mythic character "Buffalo Bill" became known to the public. Soon thereafter, Cody took control of this persona and directed its course—most of the time.

During this period Cody served as a guide for several hunting parties that came from the East out to the Great Plains. General Sheridan wanted Cody to guide these hunting parties because Cody was the best hunter and most engaging guide in the West.

The two most influential hunts for Buffalo Bill occurred during September 1871 and January 1872. The first of these Cody referred to as "General Sheridan's excursion"; members of the party were James Gorden Bennett, editor of the *New York Herald*; Charles W. Wilson, editor of the *Chicago Evening Journal*; and generals Sheridan, Hecksher, Stager, Fitzhugh, and Henry Eugene Davies. The importance of guiding this hunting party for shaping his self-image was not lost on Cody, who remarked: "Rose fresh and eager for the trip, and as it was a nobby [*sic*] and high-toned outfit which I was to accompany, I determined to put on a little style myself."[12] Moreover, General Davies wrote a sixty-eight-page pamphlet about his experiences on the hunt entitled *Ten Days on the Plains*—the first history book in which Cody, or Buffalo Bill, appears. This episode shows how Cody could use an opportunity to his advantage. Although it was General Sheridan who requested that Cody guide the party, Cody knew how to promote himself and project an heroic self-image, as General Davies recorded:

> *The most striking feature of the whole was our friend*
> *Buffalo Bill, riding down the Fort to our camp, mounted*
> *upon a snowy white horse. Dressed in a suit of light buckskin,*
> *trimmed along the seams with fringes of the same leather, his*
> *costume lighted by the crimson shirt worn under his open coat,*
> *a broad sombrero on his head, and carrying his rifle lightly in*
> *his hand, as his horse came toward us on an easy gallop, he*
> *realized to perfection the bold hunter and gallant sportsman*
> *of the plains.[13]*

In his pamphlet, published in 1871, Davies mentions Cody in such a complimentary manner that Cody wrote the following in his 1879 autobiography:

> *General Davies afterwards wrote an interesting account of this*
> *hunt and published it in a neat volume of sixty-eight pages,*

*under the title of "Ten Days on The Plains." I would have
inserted the volume bodily in this book, were it not for the fact
that the General has spoken in a rather too complimentary
manner of me.[14]*

Just as Davies's pamphlet became available to the public, the
second hunt of that winter began. This second hunt, with Grand
Duke Alexis of Russia, would put Cody's name in the world's newspapers. For this hunt, General Sheridan requested that Cody secure
the services of a party of Indians to amuse the grand duke.
Consequently, after retaining Spotted Tail's band of Sioux to pro-
vide the entertainment, Cody orchestrated a hunt that received
worldwide press coverage. At the end of the hunt Grand Duke
Alexis and General Sheridan were being driven by Cody in a "dog
cart" when General Sheridan mentioned that Cody had been a
stagecoach driver. Grand Duke Alexis wanted a demonstration,
which Cody provided, and because the coach Cody was driving had
no brakes, the ride was faster and more thrilling than any of the
men had anticipated. Grand Duke Alexis was the first of dozens of
royalty that Cody would treat to such a ride. At the end of the hunt,
Grand Duke Alexis gave several valuable presents to Cody, including a Russian fur and a pair of diamond cuff links. More importantly, however, Cody received notoriety.

After the hunt General Sheridan suggested to Cody that he visit
the East and accept some of the numerous invitations Cody had
received while guiding hunting parties. As a result, Cody traveled
to the East Coast, and the Buffalo Bill myth gained momentum.

When Cody arrived in New York, he was the hit of the social
world. At any of the many parties Cody attended, his six foot,
three-quarter inch height, cultivated voice, and genteel manners
made him an instant success. The French press lionized him as a
lady-killer. But even though he attended high-class social functions, he retained his Wild West Buffalo Bill image, showing his
appreciation of his unique status in life by wearing his buckskins
to a party and refusing to cut his hair or trade in his Stetson hat

for a top hat. After all, Cody's fame as Buffalo Bill rested on the fact that he was a scout.

As civilians, scouts were admired, even though the war being fought on the Plains was not popular because after the Civil War "Americans—at least those comfortably distant from the frontier—felt genuine sympathy for the Indian and demanded that the government policy be grounded in humanity."[15] The post-session Indian wars have been likened to Vietnam. They were both termed "police actions" by the government. The Indian wars appeared to pit mechanized might against bow and arrows when in reality "man for man, the Indian warrior far surpassed his blue-clad adversary in virtually every test of military proficiency."[16] Civilian scouts like Cody, however, were contracted by the military to get them from one place to another; they were viewed as guides, as Leather-stockings. Scouts were hired, not for the dirty, sordid business of fighting, but to lead civilization to an elevated destiny. Their dress and hairstyles were extravagant to mark them as members of this select fraternity. Thus scouts had a status with the public not given to the military in general. Other well-known figures, such as George Armstrong Custer, were also aware of the status given to scouts and changed their images accordingly as Paul Hutton remarks in an article about Custer: "Custer, ever conscious of his image, now adopted the fringed buckskin suit of the frontiersman."[17] Cody understood that his position elevated him in the eyes of society.

While Cody was in New York, Ned Buntline talked him into attending the opening night of a play Buntline had written entitled *Buffalo Bill: The King of the Border Men*. The title of this play, like those of many of the dime novels, draws a parallel between Buffalo Bill and royalty. In a society that attached importance to chivalric notions of an ideal man, this parallel is significant. It was evident that Cody had become a celebrity whom Buntline felt he could exploit. However, later events show that Buntline's knowledge of show business and the East was exploited by Cody, the westerner, to a greater extent than Buntline's use of Cody's developing

Cody in the stage costume that he wore at War Bonnet Creek. When Cody wore this costume at War Bonnet Creek, he knew that he could use it to effectively advertise himself as an actor. Courtesy of the Buffalo Bill Historical Center, Cody, Wyoming, Vincent Mercaldo Collection.

celebrity status. Cody was still unsure of his position in the East, and when his popularity was expressed by an eastern audience during the play he became embarrassed:

> *The audience, upon learning the real "Buffalo Bill" was present, gave several cheers between the acts, and I was called on to come out on the stage and make a speech…. I finally consented, and the next moment I found myself standing behind the footlights and in front of an audience for the first time in my life…. I confess that I became very much embarrassed—never more so in my life—and I knew not what to say.[18]*

Despite being offered $500 a week to play himself onstage, Cody returned to the West.

However, Buntline kept writing Cody encouraging him to return to the East, and he finally consented, secure in the knowledge that if he failed in show business he could always go back to scouting. On December16, 1872, *Scouts of the Prairie: or Red Deviltry As It Is*, written by Buntline, opened in the Chicago Amphitheatre. The play, which was poorly written since it had been hastily put together in four hours, received bad reviews from the critics. It was, however, a crowd pleaser, as many of the press notices in Cody's scrapbooks state, such as the following: "It is especially amusing to hear the whoops echo and re-echo among the gallery gods, who are in a state of ecstasy during the entire play."[19]

In the drama, Cody played an idealized version of himself as scout. This mixture of reality and idealized fiction, in addition to dime novel inventions, flattering newspaper articles, and Cody's own "leg pulling," caused many of the less sophisticated people in the audience to leave the theater convinced they had witnessed true history. This may seem absurd until we consider how the modern public's view of the historic West derives principally from stereotypic Hollywood scenarios, most of which were originally formulated for Buffalo Bill by Ned Buntline, Prentiss Ingraham, or Cody himself.

Buffalo Bill's Popularity in Show Business

IN ORDER TO BETTER UNDERSTAND WHY THE personality Buffalo Bill gained such popularity, an overview of post-Civil War America is necessary. When Cody traveled to the East in 1872, the country was settling down after the Civil War, the horrors of Reconstruction, and the impeachment proceedings of Andrew Johnson. In the defeated South the devastation was terrible:

> *The cost to the South was a quarter of a million men dead, two billion in slave property lost, and three and a half million black laborers freed. Hundreds of plantations had been devastated, and dozens of towns and cities were in ashes. Yet despite the physical and human destruction of the South, the planter's basic assumptions were intact.*[20]

This meant that in the South one-fifth of all the white males capable of carrying arms had died in the war and another one-fifth were now invalids. In her diary, Mary Chestnut remarked that the women of the South would have to come up with a new definition of male beauty because of all of the amputees. Financially, it would be a hundred years before the South recovered its antebellum economic base. Out of this suffering the southerners started a "myth of the South"[21] that glorified the Confederacy, the sterling qualities of the southern military, which "was only defeated by overwhelming odds," and reasserted antebellum southern ideals of knightly gentility and individuality. Yet as southern leaders gave lip service to these ideals, they were beginning a farm credit system that would eventually subjugate the southern masses and form a stronger feudal system than had existed before the war.

In the North, Reconstruction was not viewed any more positively than in the South. Robert Wiebe states: "Out of this process had come a haunting sense of the war's failure, a vague feeling of political betrayal."[22] Wiebe goes on to show that the North was a fragmented, suspicious society, rapidly falling under the control of businessmen. People used to the stability of a small community were thrust into an impersonal world where they felt not only insignificant but lacked the regional communal support that had buttressed them in the past. The industrial revolution demanded ever more laborers to man its front lines, and the tidal wave of immigrants made Native Americans increasingly paranoid about their security. Consequently the whole country was in a flux as,

> *expansive questions about where the country was going had elusively given way to pensive ones about where America was and who its people were. Very often this taking of stock placed the West in a position of special prominence.*[23]

Thus the assessment of new population and culture of the era created an atmosphere that made western heroes especially appealing.

Another factor that made western heroes such as Buffalo Bill widely accepted was the popularity of dime novels. Between 1861 and 1866 the Beadle and Adams publishing house sold four million of their dime novels and a million of their American Libraries editions.[24] As Albert Johannsen points out, dime novels became popular for a variety of reasons:

Dime Novels became not only household words in all sections of the country, but were the soldier's solace and comfort in camp and campaign, and contributed, in a wonderful degree, to ameliorate the trials and suffering of army life—as every yet living member of the Grand army will attest.[25]

In addition to their popularity with soldiers, dime novels were read by immigrants fresh off the boat who wished to learn about their new culture and to increase their language skills and cultural awareness—much as modern immigrants use television today. In general, the entire American public was reading light material, but according to Johannsen these novels did not start to deteriorate in quality until the 1880s, and until then the western stories "had all the earmarks of verisimilitude."[26] Not only were dime novels gaining in popularity but,

romantic fiction was becoming increasingly enticing as the appeal of respectable American writers like Hawthorne, Irving, and Longfellow waned.... In the Nineties... British and American historical romances became "a landslide millions of copies circulating among all classes except the proletariat" ... so that each season it was certain that virtually every literate American had read one such book.[27]

The need for knightly heroism was a direct consequence of the Civil War because "America, rationalistic America, progressive America, had given the world the greatest of all chivalrous wars."[28] Moreover, this pervasive need for the heroic was not entirely satisfied by fictional or sectional heroes; to some, Buffalo Bill had an even wider appeal. An unidentified newspaper wrote in 1910 that "even to-day affection for Abraham Lincoln, Ulysses S. Grant and Robert E. Lee has its sectional limitations; that of William Frederick Cody knows no boundaries."[29]

By 1876 Cody had become fairly sophisticated as a showman. Press notices stated that his acting ability was improving, and he had learned to incorporate topical news into his stage shows. This practice further confused the public concerning distinctions between the mythic and the real Buffalo Bill Cody. The best illustration of this process can be seen in connection with a well-known fight that occurred with the Indian Yellow Hand in comparison with how it was presented onstage.

The circumstances surrounding the Yellow Hand incident are complex. In the fall of 1875, Cody's best friend and Masonic brother Dr. David Franklin Powell, known as White Beaver, had experienced a painful end to his marriage, followed by excessive drinking and eventual blacklisting by the surgeon general of the military. That spring while Cody was preparing for the first act of one of his stage plays in Springfield, Massachusetts, he received a telegram that his only son Kit Carson Cody ("Kitty") lay dying of scarlet fever in the Cody home in Rochester, New York. Cody rushed home only to have Kitty die in his arms; he was devastated by the loss. By the summer the Indian wars were heating up, and Cody was called to the West to scout for his old unit, the Fifth Cavalry. Cody told his audiences that he was going off to fight Indians and arrived at Fort D. A. Russell in Cheyenne, Wyoming, on June 11, 1876. There he met General Wesley Merritt, who was taking command of the Fifth Cavalry from General Carr, a commander Cody had scouted for and respected as one of the great Indian fighters. Even though he was officially blacklisted, Powell joined up with Cody and Merritt at Fort Laramie. On the way north to meet the Fifth Cavalry, they ran into a mining party going to Deadwood, South Dakota, led by Cody's friend and mentor Wild Bill Hickok. Cody offered Hickok a job as a scout, but he and Wild Bill had a fight over dime novels written by Ned Buntline because Hickok thought that Cody was claiming to have experienced incidents from Hickok's life for personal gain. Subsequently, General Merritt and Cody met up with the Fifth Cavalry, and the troops cheered him. The Kansas *Ellis County Star* reported:

At noon on the 9th W. F. Cody (Buffalo Bill) joined the command

*as scout and guide. There is very little change in his appearance
since I saw him last in '69, except that he looks a little worn,
probably caused by his vocation in the East not agreeing with him.
All the old boys in the regiment upon seeing General Carr and
Cody together, exchanged confidences, and expressed themselves to
the effect that with such a leader and scout they could get away
with all the Sitting Bulls and Crazy Horses, in the Sioux tribe.[30]*

Cody's worn appearance mentioned by the reporter was no doubt
the result of the stress Cody had been under.

The Fifth Cavalry was heading to join with General Crook's
troops when on July 7 they got word of General Armstrong
Custer's debacle at the Little Big Horn, which had occurred on
June 25. On July 14, a report came that one thousand Cheyennes
were planning to leave the Red Cloud Agency and join the hos-
tiles in the Big Horns. General Merritt headed to cut them off.
On July 17, the Fifth Cavalry caught up to the Cheyennes at War
Bonnet Creek. Cody and General Merritt were setting a trap for
the unsuspecting Cheyennes when they had to spring it prema-
turely to save some troops who were in danger of being cut off.
Cody, who was wearing an elaborate velvet stage costume, was
several seconds ahead of the troops leading the rescue party. Also,
there was one Indian slightly ahead of the other Indian warriors.
Chris Madsen, who was the lookout for the Fifth Cavalry, reported Cody's encounter with this Indian, Yellow Hand:

*The instant they were face to face their guns fired. It seemed
almost one shot. There was no conversation, no preliminary
agreement, as has been stated erroneously in some novels written
by romantic scribes.*

*They met by accident and fired the moment they faced
each other. Cody's bullet went through the Indian's leg and
killed his pinto pony. The Indian's bullet went wild. Cody's
horse stepped into a prairie dog hole and stumbled but was
up in a moment. Cody jumped clear of his mount. Kneeling,*

Battle of Summit Springs as performed in Omaha, Nebraska. This battle, in which Cody played a significant role, became one of the mainstays of his Buffalo Bill's Wild West. *Cody grew very weary of the Yellow Hand/War Bonnet Creek fight and the image it created for him. Courtesy of the Buffalo Bill Historical Center, Cody, Wyoming.*

> *he took deliberate aim and fired the second shot. An instant before Cody fired the second shot, the Indian fired at him but missed. Cody's bullet went through the Indian's head and ended the battle. Cody went over to the fallen Indian and neatly removed his scalp.*[31]

Cody stated later that after taking Yellow Hand's scalp he raised it and declaimed, "First scalp for Custer."

Because of the scalping this incident remained a controversial event in Cody's life. It was unlike Cody to scalp a fallen foe, and he emphasized this by writing Louisa that he had taken the first scalp of his career. This encounter with Yellow Hand, along with the taking of provisions from the Cheyenne camp, represents the entire so-called Battle of War Bonnet Creek. Whatever the reason for Cody's scalping of Yellow Hand, there is no doubt that he was under a great deal of stress at the time—perhaps even unbalanced. Moreover, although the role of scout was familiar to Cody, it seems that by wearing the stage costume during the fight he was also living his new, more mythic role of Buffalo Bill.

After this incident, in spite of being made chief of scouts for the Big Horn and Yellowstone Expedition, Cody resigned to pursue show business once again:

> *There being but little prospect of any more fighting, I determined to go East as soon as possible to organize a new "Dramatic Combination" and have a new drama written for me, based upon the Sioux war. This I knew would be a paying investment, as the Sioux campaign had excited considerable interest.[32]*

The new drama that Cody had J. V. Arlington write for him was titled *The Red Right Hand; or Buffalo Bill's First Scalp for Custer.* According to Cody,

> *It was a five-act play, without head or tail, and it made no difference at which act we commenced the performance. Before we had finished the season several newspaper critics, I have been told, went crazy in trying to follow the plot. It afforded us, however, ample opportunity to give a noisy, rattling, gunpowder entertainment, and to present a succession of scenes in the late Indian war, all which seemed to give general satisfaction.[33]*

The eastern press picked up reports about the Battle of War Bonnet Creek and gave it a lot of play since during the 1876 campaign the Indian wars had not gone very well for the military: the Sioux and Cheyenne outfought General Crook's troops at the Rosebud; Custer experienced his famous defeat at the Little Big Horn; and Crook's victory at the Battle of Slim Buttes happened after Cody began performing the drama. Preshow promotion for

Buffalo Bill's latest show included a display of Yellow Hand's scalp and war accoutrements. Cody also later hired Captain Jack Crawford, who had ridden 300 miles through hostile country, and killed several mounts doing it, to bring news of victory at the Battle of Slim Buttes.

In the play, the circumstances of Cody's fight with Yellow Hand were altered for dramatic effect. The Indians were lined up on one side of the stage with the cavalry on the other side. Then Yellow Hand would step out between the two lines and offer Buffalo Bill a challenge. Buffalo Bill would accept, and they would battle with knives between two armies like ancient knights. Ultimately, Buffalo Bill would kill Yellow Hand, take his scalp, and raise it, declaiming, "First scalp for Custer," hence the play's name. This dramatization converted the minor Battle of War Bonnet Creek into an epic struggle between two knights, confusing history with fantasy. However, during his stage career, Cody was not attempting to present factual history. The plays were more like westerns, and, as Mark Siegel has stated, "Anyone who goes to the Western movie to find out the 'true story'... is likely to be disappointed."[34] Cody was capitalizing on what made him unique, and by doing so "he converted the role he was given into historical drama and ritualized legend... [he was] among the first personalitie[s] created by Americans to satisfy national anxieties and desires."[35]

A selection of press notices from Cody's 1875 to 1880 scrapbooks at the Buffalo Bill Historical Center shows some of the contributions the press made to the myth of Buffalo Bill. These press notices give Cody the qualities of an ideal chivalrous man. Sometimes they present him as a heroic but modest man: "A hero of an [sic] hundred tales, he did not even allude to himself—rather modestly declining to make himself prominent."[36] Occasionally they see him as a man who possessed a sense of humor about dangerous work: "'You have shot Indians, then, before in your life,' I asked. 'You bet your life I have,' replied William, 'I have shot and stabbed 'em, cut their bowels out with my knife, harpooned 'em, clubbed 'em to death, and in fact killed 'em in every way you can

"Card Imperial" cabinent photo of Cody circa 1885. Cabinent photos were a popular form of revenue and advertising for many events and personalities. Courtesy of the Buffalo Bill Historical Center, Cody, Wyoming.

think of, except talking 'em to death, and when I try that style I will send for you—hey Cap?'"[37] Other times they depict him as a man who is real: "Buffalo Bill is more fit to adorn the pages of a romantic reality than any fancy of the brain which could suggest... the heroes of the 'Leather stocking' tales."[38] Sometimes they portray him as an honest man: "He is a man that advertises liberally and never deceives the public."[39] Finally, they emphasize his compassion: "I [Cody] never sighted my rifle or drew my knife on an Indian but I felt almost sorry for it, and I never did it when I could help it."[40] These qualities attributed to Cody were his true qualities, but they also contributed to the ambiguity surrounding the personality of Buffalo Bill, who was presented onstage as a wholesale, cold-blooded killer of Indians, while the descriptions of Cody in the press sometimes portrayed him as sensitive and thoughtful.

The Image of Buffalo Bill in Books

THE DISTINCTION BETWEEN FACT AND FANTASY regarding the personality of Buffalo Bill was further obscured by the literature written by and about him. The dime novels about Buffalo Bill were the first books to hit the market. According to Don Russell, Buffalo Bill was the most popular character in these novels:

> "Buffalo Bill" had the largest reading following and more books written about him than any character with the exception of "Nick Carter."[41]

These dime novels usually followed a formula that depicted Buffalo Bill riding in from the wilds, having many adventures that most often involved mistaken identities, angry hunters, winsome women, cunning Indians, dastardly villains, inept soldiers, and considerable killing. The embellishment of Buffalo Bill's escapades in these books is underscored by an apology Cody once wrote to his publisher, Beadle and Adams:

> I am sorry to have to lie so outrageously in this yarn. My hero has killed more Indians on one wartrail than I have killed in all

my life. But I understand this is what is expected in border tales.
If you think the revolver and bowie-knife are used too freely, you
may cut out a fatal shot or stab wherever you deem it wise.[42]

The dime novels offered cheap entertainment, and they read
much like the screenplays of westerns.

The first of the histories and biographies championing the legend of Buffalo Bill was *The Life of the Hon. William F. Cody Known*
as Buffalo Bill, published in 1879. Cody is listed as the author, and
even though some historians have doubted the authenticity of
Cody's authorship, Don Russell believes that Cody was indeed the
author. Russell argues that no ghostwriter would have included
much of the derogatory material in this work or omitted material
that is excluded. Moreover, many stories apparently written by
Cody for this work have been documented by Russell, who states:
"By and large his original autobiography stands as our best record
of what William F. Cody thought of himself."[43]

The work reads as if Cody were sitting around a campfire,
swapping yarns and drinking whiskey. Cody portrays his early
childhood in Kansas as that of a juvenile delinquent of the Plains.
He talks about stealing apples and running away from home when
he stabbed a schoolmate in a fight over a childhood sweetheart. An
important event in Cody's childhood is the stabbing of his father
when he was giving a speech about Kansas becoming a free state.
Although Cody was present, he doesn't elaborate on his participa-
tion, and he is almost clinical in his description of this incident:

> *The fellow jumped up on the box, and pulling out a huge bowie*
> *knife, stabbed father twice, who reeled and fell to the ground.*
> *The man sprang after him, and would have ended his life then*
> *and there, had not some of the better men in the crowd*
> *interfered in time to prevent him.*[44]

Cody gives his father one short paragraph for an obituary.

As previously mentioned, because of the death of his father

Large poster of Buffalo Bill's Wild West *and "Congress of Rough Riders of the World." Posters for* Buffalo Bill's Wild West *created an enduring image of the American West. Courtesy of the Buffalo Bill Historical Center, Cody, Wyoming.*

two years later as a result of complications suffered from the stabbing Cody had to support his family, a responsibility that forced him to seek employment on the Great Plains.

While on the Plains he made many friends, the most important of which was Wild Bill Hickok. Cody states he was eleven years old when he met Hickok, who was twenty at the time. The two men were such good friends they regarded each other as brothers.[45] Most of the stories that revolve around Wild Bill deal with drinking large amounts of "tanglefoot" (whiskey) or with fistfights, shootings, and gambling. These tales have a realistic flavor because Cody writes about his sophomoric high jinks with unrefined relish. Since they scouted and "cut up" together on the Plains for fifteen years in a rough world, it is natural that the incidents reported are in an unpolished style. Cody relates stories about Hickok that can make Wild Bill appear to be a bully both on and off the Plains.

Later, Hickok joined Cody's *Buffalo Bill's Combination*. While Hickok was with the troupe, he would continually play tricks on members of the company, and he took particular delight in shooting blanks near the legs of the supers hired to be Indians for the big battles. They would jump and dance all over the stage from the burns, much to the delight of Hickok, who would laugh the whole time. In addition, while on tour Wild Bill conned people out of money and got into fights simply because local toughs bragged that they were going to "clean out" the Buffalo Bill acting company. In Cody's book, he and Hickok are portrayed as being anything but refined, but their contemporaries and friends could relate to such unrefined behavior.

One of the stories Cody is most proud of is his ride of 322 miles for the Pony Express. Cody presents this story in a straightforward manner with little embellishment. He makes no claim that it was the longest ride in Pony Express history but takes pride in the ride because it earned him the respect of Joseph Alfred Slade, his boss and at the time one of the toughest men in the West.

In relating tales, Cody reveals his predilection for self-deprecation, sometimes making himself into the butt of a joke. For example, when he tells about an exceptional series of rides he made while carrying dispatches for General Sheridan, Cody states that his mule escaped from him, and he had to chase the mule thirty-five miles back to the fort (the actual mileage, driven by the author, is about half the distance given by Cody). Once Cody got close to the fort, he heard reveille—so did the mule and brayed; Cody got mad at this effrontery and shot the mule dead. During these rides as a courier, Cody covered 355 miles in fifty-eight hours for an average of about six miles an hour through hostile territory—something all of the other scouts refused to do. This was a remarkable feat, considering it was accomplished on four horses, and a Pony Express rider was expected to cover fifteen miles an hour with a change of horses every hour.

Cody's enjoyment of a good story is evident in how he describes his life following his mother's death:

> *I entered upon a dissolute and reckless life… one day, after having been under the influence of bad whiskey, I awoke to find myself a soldier in the Seventh Kansas. I did not remember how or when I had enlisted, but I saw I was in for it, and it would not do for me to endeavor to back out.*[46]

Regarding this incident, Cody's sister, Julia Cody Goodman, states that Cody went to her husband Al for permission to enlist as Al was Cody's guardian.

In his 1879 autobiography, Cody does little to glorify himself. The battle for which he received a Congressional Medal of Honor is described in the same manner as other battles, with no mention of the award. This is not unusual as "apparently this token of honor was not particularly valued by the scouts themselves except perhaps as a token. There is little notice, in their own or others' writings, given to winning medals."[47]

For the most part Cody left the glorification of Buffalo Bill to others. He rarely read what was written about himself and would sign books without checking their contents for accuracy. Although this occurred perhaps because he was too busy, it is also true that the books helped his commercial enterprises; he might have been tempted to overlook errors that would benefit him financially.

One of the historians who contributed to the myths of Buffalo Bill and Wild Bill Hickok was James William Buel. In 1883, he published *Heroes of the Plains*, a history of several frontiersmen. This work is filled with fabrications and errors that inflate the images of Buffalo Bill and Wild Bill Hickok. For example, although Hickok and Cody were in another location, Buel places both of them in the thick of the Battle of the Washita during the 1868 to 1869 campaign—instead of General George Armstrong Custer and his troops, who attacked Black Kettle's village along the Washita River:

These two daring and intrepid scouts plunged furiously into the midst of the Indians, each with a revolver in either hand, and literally carved their way through the surging mass of red skins, leaving a furrow of dead Indians in their wake. Such fighting, such riding, and such marvelous intrepidity combined, were doubtless never equaled, and if but this act alone could be credited to the valor of Wild Bill and Buffalo Bill their names would deserve inscription on Fame's enduring monument.[48]

However, that act could not be credited to the two because they were not near the Washita River but freezing along the Republican River.

Another example of Buel's fabrication is his extension of the time period of a battle in which Cody fought. This was one of the most important battles of the Indian wars, the Battle of Summit Springs, in which Cody killed Tall Bull while serving with General Carr. Although this battle took place in a single day, Buel makes it into three separate battles.[49]

When Buel isn't making up history, he is paraphrasing Cody's 1879 autobiography and adding his own embellishments. In Buel's book, Cody's famous Pony Express ride becomes the longest in history contrary to Cody's denial of this in his autobiography; the hundred people who come out to witness a contest between Cody and Billy Comstock in Cody's autobiography become a host of several hundred in Buel's book; and Cody's own pleasantly realistic portrait of himself as a scout is transformed into a man fit to be canonized in Buel's account.

In 1888, one of the most successful of the books signed by Buffalo Bill came out: *Story of the Wild West and Campfire Chats, by Buffalo Bill (Hon. W. F. Cody): A Full and Complete History of the Renowned Pioneer Quartette, Boone, Crockett, Carson and Buffalo Bill.* In the preface to this book, Cody includes the following remarks about Carson:

I find frequent conflicts with the statements of those who in

Annie Oakley poster. Annie Oakley (Phoebe Ann Moses, or Mozee; Mrs. Frank Butler) was one of the greatest performers with a firearm who ever lived. Courtesy of the Buffalo Bill Historical Center, Cody, Wyoming.

*writing his life have made facts subservient to wild
exaggeration, just as many romancers have done while soberly
pretending to record the incidents in my own life.[50]*

Perhaps this statement is in refutation to Buel's history. Even
though Cody wrote the preface, he couldn't have read the book
because Buel's account of the Battle of Summit Springs, not
Cody's, is printed. Many of the books signed by Cody were probably ghostwritten by other people.

Cody's sister Helen Cody Wetmore ("Nellie") also contributed
significantly to the heroic myth of Buffalo Bill. From the first pages
of her book *Last of the Great Scouts: The Life Story of Col. William F.
Cody as Told by His Sister*, it is obvious that she idolized her brother.
Her saccharine style is often oppressive and, to the contemporary
reader, ludicrous. In her tales about Cody's childhood, she makes
him into a saint destined for great things. A soothsayer predicts:
"The name of this son [Cody] would be known all over the world,
and would one day be that of the President of the United States."[51]
However, the tale continues, young Cody does not want to be the
president because he knows that one day he will be the greatest
showman on earth. In Wetmore's book, Cody also fights wild animals to save his sisters. Thus she employs a motif that is endemic to
western heroes as Kent Steckmesser points out in *The Western Hero
in History and Legend*.[52] In other parts of the book, Wetmore trans-
forms her brother from a "good ol' boy" to a saint. According to
her, Cody took one drink of hard cider and swore off it forever,
although it apparently did not stop him from drinking whiskey.
And when Cody started to work for the freighting firm of Russell,
Majors, and Waddell, she reports he took the following pledge:

*I, William F. Cody, …do hereby solemnly swear, before the
great and living God, that during my engagement with, and
while I am in the employ of, Russell, Majors and Waddell, I
will under no circumstances, use profane language, that I will
not quarrel or fight with any other employee of the firm, and*

that in every respect I will conduct myself honestly, be faithful to my duties, and so direct all my acts as to win the confidence of my employers. So help me God.[53]

In Wetmore's book, the death of Cody's father as a result of being stabbed, which gets little coverage and is treated as insignificant in Cody's autobiography, becomes a major event and a part of Kansas history known as "The Cody Bloody Trail." Moreover, Cody's sister states that Cody swore revenge and eventually got it during the Civil War.

Whenever Wild Bill Hickok makes one of his few brief appearances in Wetmore's book, she calls him Colonel Hickok—without mentioning when and where Hickok got promoted from scout to colonel. For the most part, however, Wild Bill remains in the background of her book, an unimportant character.

Another fallacy of Wetmore's book is that it depicts Cody as having made the longest Pony Express ride in history—a record actually attained by "Pony Bob" Haslam, who was employed by Cody. Although "Pony Bob" made the longest ride in Pony Express history during the Paiute War, Wetmore wrote about Cody: "There was no rest for the rider, but twenty-one horses were used on the run—the longest ever made by a Pony Express rider."[54]

Cody's sister also made free use of her brother's autobiography when it suited her purpose, but she avoided any story that might denigrate him—like Cody's enlistment in the Union Army while drunk. Consequently, her book depicts a demigod who grew up on the Plains, not a "natural gentleman" capable of incredible feats of endurance and strength. Although by presenting Cody as a paragon of virtue Wetmore set her brother on a pedestal as an example for children to emulate, ironically some of her incorrect statements would eventually be used to discredit Buffalo Bill.

Buffalo Bill's Wild West

CERTAINLY ONE OF THE PRINCIPAL FACTORS THAT contributed to the enduring myth of Buffalo Bill in the annals of history was *Buffalo Bill's Wild West*. *Buffalo Bill's Wild West* lasted thirty years, from May 19, 1883, until it was auctioned off on July 21, 1913. Cody's scrapbooks are full of notices representing tens of thousands of free passes for children. He felt that *Buffalo Bill's Wild West* was an educational exhibit, and he was teaching the world about the West.

In analyzing the mythic elements of *Buffalo Bill's Wild West*, several facets must be addressed: the publicity, the presentation itself, the literature that was sold with it, and the public's perception of the show.

Cody's press agent, Arizona John Burke, kept the name, image, and concept of his idol Colonel William F. "Buffalo Bill" Cody in the forefront of public awareness. Burke has been called the greatest press agent of his age, and he knew every newspaper editor by name once he had been introduced.[55] Burke, who did not write well because of his predilection for using a large number of adjectives to the exclusion of other parts of speech, had the uncanny knack of getting editors and other writers to gush about Buffalo Bill after hearing his fanciful stories built on Cody's factual

Older formal cabinent photo of Cody circa 1885. Courtesy of the Buffalo Bill Historical Center, Cody, Wyoming.

exploits. Like Ned Buntline, Prentiss Ingraham, Fredrick Remington, William Cody, and occassional others who worked with *Buffalo Bill's Wild West*, Burke painted a portrait of the American West using his own medium.

There was usually considerable and sometimes extravagant publicity for *Buffalo Bill's Wild West*. The number of posters that were posted for a one-night stand of *Buffalo Bill's Wild West* averaged between six and eight thousand of varying quality and sizes. Posters came in "sheets" that measured 28 inches by 42 inches, and billboards would be put up with images generally ranging in size from a half sheet to thirty-two sheets. Larger images of forty-eight and sixty-four were not unheard of, and *Buffalo Bill's Wild West* occasionally used posters of one hundred sheets or more.[56] The more spectacular scenes of eight sheets and above were usually kept for larger cities, where *Buffalo Bill's Wild West* stayed longer. *Buffalo Bill's Wild West* posters were the best of the era, and because they were the most effective way of attracting crowds, cities were plastered with them, and their romanticized images were burned into the public's consciousness. A London *Globe* commentator remarked of the inundation of posters of Cody in 1887:

> *I may walk it, or 'bus it, or hansom it: still*
> *I am faced by the features of Buffalo Bill.*
> *Every hoarding [billboard] is plastered, from*
>   *East-end to West*
> *With his hat, coat, and countenance, lovelocks*
>   *and vest.*[57]

What made *Buffalo Bill's Wild West* unique was the exhibition of various elements of the American West. In the animal pens were elk, deer, mountain sheep, hundreds of horses, mules, and, of course, one of the few remaining buffalo herds in the world. Starting with the 1893 Columbian Exposition in Chicago, the crowd could view the cabin in which Sitting Bull had been killed, "embalming the memory of the dead chief."[58] At the Indian villages, one could see entire family groups because Cody had paid each brave $15 a month extra for each wife and $5 a month extra for each child he brought with him. Cody only paid extra for the families of the Indians, whom he referred to as "the first Americans," and he did this so the viewing public could see that Indians were like everybody else.[59]

After the 1892 season in London, Cody hired other novelty acts from around the world to keep the show fresh. Ethnic units were kept together so that if individuals were interested in seeing specific peoples they could go to where the peoples were located. At various times after the 1892 season until *Buffalo Bill's Wild West* was auctioned off, an audience member could see Cossacks, Riffs, Samurai, gauchos, and vaqueros; the elite cavalry units of France, Germany, England, and the United States; cowboys, frontiersmen, Indians, and, of course, Buffalo Bill himself. An important aspect of the show was the veracity the audience could experience. Cody stated at a dinner party in Florence, Italy, that "the men ... with us are those who have actually taken part in the scenes they represent."[60] After 1902, when his partner was the circus showman James A. Bailey, *Buffalo Bill's Wild West* had side shows. In addition, throughout the thirty years of *Buffalo Bill's Wild West*, audience members often had the opportunity to see royalty and celebrities on the arena grounds.

Once seated in the covered, three-quarter rectangular grandstand, the audience would first listen to "The Star Spangled Banner" and then watch Cody's presentation, a great variety of reenactments of Wild West activities and events. The fact that it was a realistic show was often attested to by the visiting generals, frontiersmen, and writers. One of the most notable writers to attend was Mark Twain, a friend of Cody's, who wrote:

> *Down to its smallest details, the show is genuine—cowboys, vaqueros, Indians, stage coach, costumes and all; it is wholly free from sham and insincerity and the effects it produced upon*

*me by its spectacles were identical with those wrought upon me
a long time ago by the same spectacles on the frontier. Your pony
expressman was as tremendous an interest to me as he was
twenty-three years ago when he used to come whizzing by from
over the desert with his war news; your bucking horses were
even painfully real to me as I rode one of those outrages for
nearly a quarter of a minute. It is often said on the other side
of the water that none of the exhibitions which we send to
England are purely and distinctly American. If you will take
the Wild West Show over there you can remove that
reproach.*[61]

What the public saw varied slightly from season to season as
Cody would modify the spectacle so the show remained fresh and
topical. However, the basic format is stated in the following
"Programme" of the 1885 season:

1. *Grand Processional Parade.*
2. *Entree. Introduction of characters, groups and bands.*
3. *Race between Cow-Boy, Mexican, and Indian.*
4. *Pony Express by Billy Johnson.*
5. *100-yard race between Indian Pony and Indian on Foot.*
6. *Duel between Buffalo Bill and Yellow Hand.*
7. *Rifle Shooting by Seth Clover.*
8. *Master Johnny Baker, the Cow-Boy Kid.*
9. *Miss Annie Oakley, Champion Lady Shot.*
10. *Miss Lillian Smith. The California Huntress Champion Shot.*
11. *The Cow-Boy's Fun, or Riding of Bucking Ponies and
    Mules, by Buck Taylor, Bronco Bill, Bill Bullock, Tim
    Clayton, Coyote Bill, Bridle Bill.*
12. *Hon. Wm. F. Cody (Buffalo Bill), America's Practical
    All-Round-Shot, Shooting with Rifle, Shot Gun, and
    Revolver, on Foot and Horseback.*
13. *The Deadwood Stage Coach.*
14. *Race between Sioux Boys on Bareback Indian Ponies.*

15. *Race between Mexican Thoroughbreds.*
16. *War, Grass, Corn, and Scalp Dances, by Pawnee, Wichita, and Sioux Indians.*
17. *Race between Lady Riders.*
18. *Mustang Jack (Pets-ze-ca-we-cha-cha), the Great Jumper.*
19. *Roping and Riding of Wild Texas Steers, by Cow-Boys and Mexicans.*
20. *Hunting of Buffalo, by Buffalo Bill, Cow-Boys and Mexicans.*
21. *Riding of Wild Elk by Voter Hall.*
22. *Attack on Settlers' Cabin by Indians, and Repulsed by BUFFALO BILL, Cow-Boys, and Mexicans. SALUTE.*

The name Buffalo Bill is lightly highlighted in the program, not because of Cody's ego (he was a modest man by all accounts) but because he was the main attraction. As the Troy, New York, *Daily Item* put it: "To use a time honored expression, without Buffalo Bill the show would be Hamlet with Hamlet left out."[62] Since this meant Cody always had to show up, it had its drawbacks as well as its glory for a man of Cody's integrity. During the 1908 to 1909 season, newspapers often quoted Cody as stating that he had only missed nine performances in his first twenty-six years as a showman. That Buffalo Bill would be at the performance was one of the things the public could count on when they went to *Buffalo Bill's Wild West*. And that Cody felt an obligation to the public is clear from one of his statements:

> *I believe in keeping faith with the public and if I was to take a holiday for a week or even a couple of days, people would come to the show and they might think they weren't getting value for their money. They might say "Where's Buffalo Bill? He's part of the entertainment, and I paid to see him." If I was away on my own pleasure they'd have every right to complain.*[63]

To better understand Cody's popularity in *Buffalo Bill's Wild West*, it is necessary to look at the history of American theater during Cody's time. When Cody started his theatrical career, the American theater was in transition. During the middle of the nineteenth century American taste was still under the influence of P. T. Barnum, whose brand of showmanship was to "humbug" the audience and let them guess how he did it.

Theater tended to be melodramatic and unrefined, with considerable interaction between the actors and the audience. As Kathy Peiss writes: "Theater-goers prompted actors, hissed villains, and warned heroines of oncoming danger, creating a sense of identity between the performers and the members of the audience."[64]

By the 1870s, however, there was a movement to clean up theaters and plays, remove the prostitutes from the top balcony, and to make the entertainment suitable for the entire family. The melodramas Cody acted in were loud, wholesome spectacles that everyone could enjoy.

During the 1880s, Cody's dramas became more sophisticated—a change that paralleled the general trend in theater. When Cody made his stage debut in 1872, however, the "gallery gods" weren't interested in plot, characterization, or thematic content; they were not interested in illusion but in seeing reality onstage. Cody became a stage celebrity initially because of the reality he presented. He had actually lived the roles he played onstage, and this had a great attraction for his audience. This was underscored by the fact that in the course of his stage career, Cody would spend the winters touring with stage productions and the summers scouting on the Plains. When *Scouts of the Prairie* first opened, Cody was well known because of his work as a scout. The titles of Cody's first and second shows, *Scouts of the Plains*, reinforced his stature and announced to the audience exactly what they were going to see. Cody himself later stated: "I didn't try to act—I did what I used to do on the prairie, not what I thought some other fellow might have done if he felt that way."[65] Cody also stated to a Glasgow, Scotland, newspaper that during a show in Texas he decided it would be fun to play the show backwards and see if the audience noticed anything wrong; they didn't.[66]

What the audience came to see was a "knight" of the Plains; indeed, one of Cody's later shows was titled *Knight of the Plains*, and Cody played the role to a tee because he *was* what the audience wanted to see.

The use of special effects added to the appeal of the shows and thus to the Buffalo Bill myth. Stage machinery was becoming more sophisticated, allowing for realistic stage effects that could be startling for the audience, as they were for Wild Bill Hickok when he first saw his friend Cody onstage. In her *Memoirs of Buffalo Bill by His Wife*, Cody's wife Louisa quoted Hickok as saying the following when he saw Cody with limelight on him, which gives one an otherworldly appearance: "'For the sake of Jehosophat what's that Bill Cody's got on him out there? Boy run just as fast as your legs will carry you and get me five dollars worth of that stuff, I want it smeared all over me.'"[67]

In addition to special effects, Cody would impress the audience with dramatic, unconventional actions like picking up "dead" supernumeraries with one hand and lightly carrying them offstage, using real horses and real Indians, and shooting apples from the heads and dollars from the hands of audience members. Those audience members with a perverse sense of values could hope for injuries among the cowboys and horses, which happened regularly, or an arm or two being blown off during the artillery drill, which happened twice.[68] At these times fantasy would meld into reality with shocking clarity. Other times Cody would also break with stage tradition and give impromptu curtain speeches such as when he spotted his wife in the audience of DeBar's Opera House in St. Louis. On that evening, Cody walked to the footlights and shouted out, "Oh, Mama, I'm a bad actor… honest Mama, does this look as awful out there as it feels up here?"[69] But despite the special effects and dramatic actions, Cody's performances onstage did not seem deceptive or contrived because he relaxed and had a good time. The shows, however, were far from factual.

Louisa Cody around the time of her marriage to William. Cody had not known many women before he met Louisa and was captivated by her. Courtesy of the Buffalo Bill Historical Center, Cody, Wyoming.

When Cody started *Buffalo Bill's Wild West*, the arena allowed him to show a greater number of his talents than he had been able to do in regular theatrical dramas. Cody was a superb horseman whom the British press recommended their readers view to get a lesson in horsemanship. A centaur was a simile often used to describe Cody by the world's press. Although Cody employed people who could target shoot better than him, even Luther North, who after Cody's death was one of his biggest detractors, wrote: "I want to say here that the man never lived that could equal him shooting with a rifle from the back of a galloping horse... he was in a class by himself."[70]

Cody managed to fuse an idealized concept of manhood with the world's positive emotional response to the frontier. Cody was acceptable as a mythic hero because he stood for the values of southern individualism as well as northern industrial pragmatism. He helped the government kill Indians, whose holistic spiritualism did not mesh with the white man's scientific positivism. At the same time, Cody didn't offend the Indians, who respected him for always treating them fairly and not using his influence to persuade them to sign treaties of dubious value.[71] Moreover, it was well known that Cody's best friend and frequent companion Dr. David Franklin "White Beaver" Powell was a mixed-blood Seneca. The ambiguities in Cody's life fitted perfectly with the ambiguous nature of the frontier literary hero—an enigma that helps to civilize the frontier and then retreats to the wilds. The public read of Cody's heroics on the Plains in dime novels, history books, and newspapers, and the knightly virtues ascribed to Buffalo Bill were reinforced firsthand by the superb way Cody handled horses and firearms. In Buffalo Bill the frontier mythic framework merged with an individual who actually embodied the myth. This was the basis of Buffalo Bill's huge success.

During the 1886 winter season, *Buffalo Bill's Wild West* was playing Madison Square Garden in a pageant called *The Drama of Civilization*, which opened the evening before Thanksgiving. Steele MacKaye had written the scenario, which was in five acts:

William Cody, Frank Powell, and a rifle team during a 1887 trip to London. Frank Powell frequently traveled with Cody, consequently missing over half of the city council meetings during his first term as mayor of La Crosse, Wisconsin, in 1885. Courtesy of the Buffalo Bill Historical Center, Cody, Wyoming.

"The Primeval Forest," "The Prairie," "The Cattle Ranch," "The Mining Camp," and "Custer's Last Stand." There were spectacular effects designed by Matt Morgan, Nelse Waldron, and Lew Parker, but the highlight of the show was "Custer's Last Stand." In this act, six-foot-four-inch Buck Taylor (The King of the Cowboys) played Custer, and the audience could vicariously relive the events of 1876. After the defeat, the Indians would leave the tableau of the dead Seventh Cavalry; then Cody would enter, and the lights would flash "Too Late." Next, Yellow Hand and his band of Cheyennes would come on, and the Battle of War Bonnet Creek would be reenacted just as it had been in the previous stage show, only on a grander scale. The finale of this drama underscored Cody's importance—both as a fighter of the Indian wars

Cody in a "line-up" shot. As Cody got older, photos sold with Buffalo Bill's Wild West revealed that Buffalo Bill's paint and thinning hair had started to show. Courtesy of the Sorg Collection.

and as a heroic, mythic individual. Because of the dramatic lead up, it appeared to the audience that if Cody had been at the Little Big Horn, Custer might have survived the battle. This scenario also left Cody onstage in the final scene—as the end product of the "drama of civilization." If Cody's presence alone was not enough to raise Buffalo Bill to a mythic level, there were special effects, such as prairie fires, cyclones, locomotives, enormous backdrops, and elaborately painted scenery to enhance the effect.

In the programs that sold with *Buffalo Bill's Wild West*, there was a marked trend toward portraying the truth about Cody. Quotations from army officers and the press, as well as a factual biography, gave Cody all the status he needed. The other white performers were given titles and short inflated biographies to make them appear of the same caliber as Buffalo Bill. Only the Indians received nearly as much space in the programs as Cody. Since the Indians in *Buffalo Bill's Wild West* we· ieaders of their people, the simple truth provided sufficient prestige. The names of these Indians, such as Iron Tail, Curly, Red Shirt, and American Horse, had been in the newspapers frequently enough for the public to have heard of at least some of them. Some of the programs also attempted to educate whites about the true nature of Indians. Cody had an insert put in the 1893 program pleading for just and humane treatment of Indians—stating that Indians make good soldiers, farmers, and citizens if they are given a chance. Thus the programs expressed hopes for better understanding between the races.

Cody felt that *Buffalo Bill's Wild West* was an educational show because it presented to the public unusual people and lifestyles. The show focused on the spectacular rather than the mundane. As a reporter for the *Stamford Telegram* noted: "Col. Cody became an educator in one of the most interesting and least familiar fields of human experience."[72]

Through *Buffalo Bill's Wild West*, the myth of Buffalo Bill was reinforced and perpetuated. Eventually, however, the image of Buffalo Bill became tainted by imitators—men without the

716. - PARIS. - Panorama du Champ de Mars et Buffalo. - G. I.

Paris show grounds Champ de Mars. In addition to coverage as a performer, the French press lionized Cody as a great womanizer; this type of press coverage did little to help the Codys' marriage. Courtesy of the Buffalo Bill Historical Center, Cody, Wyoming.

credentials, who, like Pawnee Bill and Doc Carver, made up lies to avoid being in the shadow of Buffalo Bill. Such imitators produced dramas of events that were of inferior quality and which reflected negatively on *Buffalo Bill's Wild West*. The *Lussire News* of England correctly predicted the degeneration of the Buffalo Bill myth: "The business will degenerate into the hands of men devoid of Buffalo Bill's exalted simplicity, and much more eager to finger the shillings of the public than to shake the hand of mother Nature." Although there were other factors that contributed to the downfall of Buffalo Bill, the main one was men "eager to finger the shillings" of William Cody.

Part 2

The Reality: William F. Cody

William Cody's Private Life

By ALL ACCOUNTS WILLIAM CODY WAS EVERYBODY'S friend, a guileless egalitarian who treated all people equal regardless of race or social stature. Unfortunately, this made him vulnerable to the agendas of unscrupulous businessmen. Cody's sense of obligation to his family is seen in his promise to his dying mother that he would take care of his siblings financially. Even before, when the Cody children were growing up, William assumed his father's duties and his sister Julia the duties of their mother.

The Cody family was split into various factions. Cody's sister Julia was his close friend and confidante, and in his letters to her he frequently asked her not to divulge information to the other family members. Cody was also very friendly with Julia's husband, Al, often addressing him as "brother Al" in his letters. There is little doubt that, of all his immediate family, Cody was closest to these two people. The intimate friendship that Cody shared with them caused friction with other family members, including his wife, Louisa, who was jealous of any other person's relationship with Cody.

Julia and Al were trusted friends whom Cody could depend on to help with his business affairs. After Cody started his successful stage career, Al and Julia managed his Scout's Rest Ranch, which would have operated in the black if Cody had not used it as a convalescent home for performers injured in *Buffalo Bill's Wild West*, as well as a dude ranch for the numerous guests Cody entertained. Cody left most of the ranch management to Al and only made suggestions. Julia had charge of the ranch's house, which had an oven built by Al capable of baking thirty-five loaves of bread simultaneously to accommodate the large number of people who often stayed there.[1]

Helen ("Nellie") seems to have been the biggest financial burden of Cody's sisters. Cody bought the Duluth Press for Helen and her husband, Hugh, because Helen had complained that Cody did not take care of her. Cody also gave the couple a contract to print Helen's book *Buffalo Bill: Last of the Great Scouts*. Cody's other sisters, May and Lida, were apparently a minor drain on the Cody finances and were content to live their own lives.

Three of Cody's children died before Cody: Orra Maude and Kit Carson ("Kitty") died in childhood, and Arta died shortly after her second marriage to Charles Thorp in 1904. Arta lived a private life, but according to existing records she had a very unhappy marriage with her first husband, Horton Boal. Although Cody and Dr. Frank (White Beaver) Powell kept Boal employed in several of their various enterprises, Boal probably felt subservient and powerless, and he committed suicide in Cody's Sheridan Inn in late 1902. The only one of Cody's children who survived him was Irma, the youngest, who sided with her father during her parents' estrangement and divorce hearing in the early 1900s. Cody frequently took her hunting, and Irma visited him while he was on tour.

Very often Dr. Powell, Cody's blood brother (as Cody referred to him) was by his side—in good times as well as bad. When Cody went to the Standing Rock Reservation during the winter of 1890 to arrest Sitting Bull, an assignment called "the most dangerous mission the government ever asked [him] to perform," he wanted Powell to join him because, as Cody put it, "we've been through it before."[2] And even though Powell was an active politician and twice ran for governor in Wisconsin, a lot of the time he was present to share Cody's triumphs.

Some members of Cody's immediate family as well as his ward, Johnny Baker, who started tagging along with *Buffalo Bill's Wild West* from the beginning, and his general manager, "Arizona" John M. Burke, tended to deify Cody. Along with the public, they saw Cody unrealistically and placed him on a lofty pedestal. However, Julia, Al, and Dr. Powell saw Buffalo Bill in a realistic light. The relationships among these four are the relationships of adults comfortable with each other.

Of the many stories concerning how Cody met his wife, Louisa, the most characteristic and colorful one is that during the Civil War Cody was on leave visiting a friend named William McDonald, who invited Cody to see his cousin Louisa. When they arrived, they found her asleep in a chair in front of a fire. Cody snuck up behind her, jerked the chair out from underneath her, and she jumped up and hit him in the face. They got married about a year later. Louisa, who had been educated in a convent and was called Lulu, must have fascinated Cody, who was nineteen years old at the time. Lulu's book *Memories of Buffalo Bill by His Wife* is like a gothic romance with Lulu as the heroine. She sees herself as a lady and Cody as a knight errant. The book focuses mostly on their life together on the Plains when Cody would save her from real or imagined danger. Unfortunately, one of the things that caused a rift between them was Lulu's lack of interest in, and disapproval of, show business. Drinking and show business were very sinful to many Catholics, and Lulu did not understand the pageantry involved in it. Consequently, when Cody toured the country with his shows Lulu usually stayed at home, uncomfortable with the proposition of sharing Cody with all his fans.

Lulu's reluctance to travel with *Buffalo Bill's Wild West* was also the result of an incident that occurred during the 1875 season, when the theatrical combination closed in California. Lulu was traveling with the company for the last part of the tour. It had been a highly successful season both financially and socially—

Kit Carson Cody. "Kitty" was the apple of his father's eye, and his death reportedly triggered William and Louisa's estrangement. Cody wanted to have the family name carried on, and Kitty's death may have influenced Cody's paternalistic philanthropy. Courtesy of the Buffalo Bill Historical Center, Cody, Wyoming.

everybody ended up on friendly terms, calling Cody "Papa" and "Old Man." The company had a little party, and the women all came up to Cody and were kissing him in a harmless way when Lulu walked in and became jealous.

Another major event that caused friction in the Cody marriage was that their only son, Kit Carson ("Kitty") Cody, died of scarlet fever in 1876. Beata Cox of North Platte, who knew Lulu for eleven years, said Lulu told her that "Willie [had] gotten wild and 'fast' after Kit's death, and she [Lulu] began finding other women in their bedroom. Because of this she would not travel with him anymore, 'but it never would've happened if [their] boy had lived.'"[3]

An additional factor that contributed to their rocky marriage was Lulu's double dealings about land, which began around the time of Kitty's death. Cody would often send money home for Lulu to buy more land for the ranch; she did but put it all in her own name. When Lulu died, she was worth $95,000, and when Cody died he was facing debts of over $150,000; $20,000 would have kept Cody solvent in 1913. In 1882, when Cody found out that Lulu was putting property in her name, he wrote Julia the following letter, which expresses the degree of estrangement between the couple:

I am in a peck of trouble. What do you think? Lulu has got most if not all of our North Platte property in her name.... And she says what she has got she is going to hold on to. Now what do you think of that? Ain't that a nice way for a wife to act? Who was a pauper when I married her and [sic] I have supported her parents for nearly sixteen years. I have been sending money to her for the last five years to buy property, not dreaming but what she was buying it in my name but instead she had it put in her name, and now claims it. Would you have thought that of Lulu? After all these years of my working for her. I don't care a snap for the money, but the way she has treated me. My beautiful house. I have none to go to. Al and I will have to build another.[4]

Ultimately, this estrangement between Cody and Lulu culminated in a divorce hearing in 1904 when Cody wanted their marriage disolved.

After postponements and a change of venue from Sheridan to Cheyenne, Wyoming, the divorce hearing began on February 16, 1905, with Judge R. H. Scott presiding. The hearing attracted the press and did a lot to tarnish Cody's reputation. Cody accused Lulu of trying to poison him on two occasions and complained that Lulu was rude to his guests and a nag to him. Lulu accused Cody of having affairs with several women, including Queen Victoria. Finally, Judge Scott threw the case out of court. Although they eventually reconciled on July 28, 1910, the hearing had shown the American public another, less heroic side to Cody they had not seen on the Plains or onstage. In spite of all the trouble between Cody and Lulu, she stood by him during his final years and stated after he died: "He is still my ideal—yes and my idol."[5]

William Cody's Business Ventures

EVEN THOUGH CODY IS KNOWN PRIMARILY FOR HIS exploits on the Plains and his presentations of *Buffalo Bill's Wild West*, he was also involved in numerous business ventures of varying success. Many of these ventures were connected with the development of the West:

> *Every cent that I have made in the show business I have invested in the West in developing the arid plains that are now fine home lands peopled with happy American families. Once I spent $700,000 in digging an irrigation canal before I got a cent returned. Some of the land I bought then for $2 an acre I sold last week for $480 an acre, but then I hung on to it, don't you see.*[6]

Unfortunately, Cody never was able to hold onto the profits from his investments. Some businesses were not profitable because they were too diverse, paid small (if any) returns, were subject to government interference, or their managers cheated Cody. Other times, Cody simply gave profits from businesses to individuals or charitable causes. If Cody had saved only 25 percent of the money he spent on the irrigation canal at Cody,

Wyoming, he might have avoided financial ruin at the end of his life. But despite his financial problems, Cody was a man whom even his critics, such as historian Richard J. Walsh, admired. Cody's true greatness was reflected in what he did with the estimated $3 million he made as a showman and the courage with which he faced the final years of his life.

The biggest single drain on Cody's fortune was his twentieth-century Arizona mining project Oracle:

> *It was an "Old Friend," a scout named Captain Burgess, who knew Colonel Cody, better known as Buffalo Bill in the Indian war days on the western plains, persuaded his old friend to take a flyer in the mining game. Under its new ownership Campo Bonito soared into glamorous distinction.*[7]

Campo Bonito may have soared to "glamorous distinction," but when Cody got involved in the mining business his finances took a turn for the worse:

> *On the advice of an old friend Cody formed a syndicate composed of Cody, Burgess, and Getchell and turned six claims at Campo Bonito into a $600,000 corporation under the style and title of the Campo Bonito Mining Company.*[8]

Another partner was Colonel D. B. Dyer, and with him Cody established the Cody-Dyer Mining and Milling Company.

At the time of purchase, the mines had a potential daily profit of $2,000, but soon the profits plummeted due to bad management decisions. The syndicate hired a man named Sherman, who was reportedly a high-powered mining engineer, to manage the mines. When Sherman took over the mines, they were profitable, but he decided they needed to be closed so that they could be modified for increased production. As a result, soon Cody was employing three hundred men to work the forty-five claims listed with the company by June 1911. Moreover, Cody's partners, who should have been protecting his interests, were actually soaking him by padding the payrolls, double charging for equipment, and often buying nearby claims and selling them to the company at ten times the cost. Eventually, Cody became suspicious and sent his nephew E. J. Ewing to investigate. Ewing told Cody he was being taken, and Cody was about to close operations when scheelite, raw tungsten, was found. It was not until after Cody's death that the mines eventually provided $10,000 worth of tungsten for the country's war efforts. Newspaper articles in the Buffalo Bill Historical Center's scrapbooks and the Tucson Public Library files indicate that the mines were going to pay off at any moment. It is possible that the mines were salted—phony ore deposited in them to make the mines look valuable. Whatever the case, Cody poured approximately half a million dollars down the Oracle mineshafts without seeing any profits.

Cody should have known better since the Arizona mines were not his first experience with mines that were probably salted. At the turn of the century, Buffalo Bill's "blood brother," Dr. Frank (White Beaver) Powell, owned a mining claim in Grand Encampment, Wyoming. The newspaper articles in the *Grand Encampment Herald* about Dr. Powell's Copper Giant Gold and Copper Mining Company are very similar in their optimistic tone to the Arizona articles about Cody's mines a decade later. Like Cody, Powell invested good money after bad when such optimistic articles appeared in the paper, and Dr. Powell soon found himself broke. He turned to Cody for help, who bailed him out by purchasing $60,000 worth of Copper Giant stock. When the Copper Giant continued to show nothing but promise, Cody closed down the operation. Unfortunately, Cody did not show the same business acumen with his Arizona mines.[9]

The government also contributed to the depletion of Cody's fortune. During his scouting career, Cody saw the tourism and agricultural possibilities of the area east of Yellowstone National Park. In the early 1890s, Cody and George Washington Beck

Cody watering his horse during a performance of Buffalo Bill's Wild West. Buffalo Bill's Wild West *presented some scenarios that would appear very mundane to modern audiences. Courtesy of the Buffalo Bill Historical Center, Cody, Wyoming.*

decided to establish a development in the region, which in a few years became Cody, Wyoming—named after its founder. To obtain the land segregation (exclusive right to develop) for the area that became Cody, Wyoming, Buffalo Bill promised the government he would irrigate it. Much of the $700,000 that Cody invested in the irrigation system at Cody, Wyoming, was lost when the federal government pressured Cody into releasing his land segregation and letting them build the Shoshone Dam—now the Buffalo Bill Dam. Cody owned much of the land now covered by water. In exchange for building the dam, the government promised Cody to extend the canal that Cody's Shoshone Land and Irrigation Company had started to construct. Although the government did this, in the process the terminus of the canal was moved from Ralston, Wyoming, which was owned by Cody and General Miles, to Powell, Wyoming, twelve miles away. As a result, Ralston went from a boomtown to only a stage stop between Cody and Powell, Wyoming. Even though Cody and General Miles lost a lot of money due to the economic decline of Ralston, this apparently did not bother Cody, whose sole concern expressed in his letters was "for the best interest of the state."[10]

Cody's overriding interest in developing Wyoming meant in many cases giving away land. When a large Mormon colony wanted to settle in the area, Cody relinquished part of his company's segregation along the Shoshone River. This irritated Nate Salsbury, Cody's business partner, who thought they could have gotten $20,000 for the land. Cody's reply illustrates his generosity: "When you die it will be said of you 'here lies Nate Salsbury who made a million dollars in the show business and kept it,' but when I die people will say, 'Here lies Bill Cody, who made a million dollars in the show business and distributed it among his friends.'"[11]

Cody's philanthropic bent and concern for humanity influenced many of his business decisions. In his letters concerning DeMaris Springs outside of Cody, Wyoming, Cody indicated he wanted the supposed medicinal water bottled and sold at cost around the country for the "benefit of humanity."[12] The *Cody Enterprise*, founded by Cody, states that from March 1, 1901, to December 1, 1902, Cody spent $216,500 to develop the new town. And in order to interest the Burlington Railroad in building a spur to Cody, Wyoming, Cody and his partners gave the railroad half of their land, also promising to build two hotels on the road to Yellowstone and contribute to construction of the road, the cost of which was $50,000. Although Cody may have learned his lesson about greasing the proper palms since the time he had founded the town of Rome, Kansas, he invested a considerable sum of money in building his town of Cody without realizing any profit.

In 1900, Cody estimated that he had 4,000 men working for him developing his Wyoming properties in addition to the approximately 650 people employed in *Buffalo Bill's Wild West*. Cody had vast property holdings and numerous businesses partly because of the larger role he saw himself playing in society: Buffalo Bill did "not wish to be only known as a scout and show-man, but as a pioneer and developer of civilization."[13] By 1910, Cody owned the following businesses: the Campo Bonito Mining and Milling Company, the Southern Belle Mining Company, the Cody Coal Company, and the Shoshone Irrigation Company; a 4,000-acre and an 800-acre farm in North Platte, Nebraska, and five farms near Cody, Wyoming; the Irma Hotel, Pahaska Tepee, and Wapiti Inn; and two horse and cattle ranches. In addition, Cody had invested heavily in the Cody Oil Fields; had large realty holdings in Duluth, Minnesota, and in La Crosse, Wisconsin; had interests in several copper mines in southwestern Wyoming; and was the founder of the Montezuma Oil Company of Arizona. Other interests he had at one time or another were: a sulfur plant in Cody, Wyoming; an irrigation project he completed in North Platte, Nebraska; an irrigation project in Arizona; and the Sheridan Inn in Sheridan, Wyoming. Moreover, before his good friend Dr. Powell died in 1906 they promoted or owned: the Multiple Railway System; the Copper Giant Gold and Copper Mining Corporation; Yosemite Yarrow Cough Cream and Wonder Worker; White Beaver's Cough Cream—The Great Lung Healer; and Panamalt (a sub-stitute for alcoholic beverages and coffee).

Very few of these businesses operated in the black because Cody was either being cheated, was too visionary, or used his property to entertain guests in a lavish manner. Cody was honest and assumed other people were honest. Regarding Cody's finan-cial matters being shaky, Nate Salsbury wrote the following to Cody after visiting Cody, Wyoming:

> *[You are] carrying a lot of "little" things and a lot of little people in the Big Horn Basin that will eat up every dollar you can get for the rest of your life if you don't get rid of them.*

When I was in the Big Horn Basin I saw your affairs conducted in a way that made me sick to my stomach. And from what I hear they are no better now.[14]

Typically, Cody's reaction to warnings of financial disaster was to lose sleep and write letters to his managers requesting information. However, the following letter to his sister, Julia, written about the time of Salsbury's warning, reveals how financial problems were secondary to humanitarian concerns:

No one wants to do right more then I do and I propose to lead an honest life—doing good helping my fellow creature when and wherever I can. And I will do all the good I can while on earth. wronging [sic] no one knowingly, and will try to make every one else better than I am myself, restrain vice & wickedness whenever I can, help the poor and needy.[15]

Cody's writings are filled with similar quixotic but humanitarian visions. And it was often Cody's generosity that undermined his financial security. For example, when *Buffalo Bill's Wild West* performances at the 1893 Columbian Exposition netted Cody and his partner Nate Salsbury approximately $1 million, Cody reportedly paid off the debts of the six local churches in his hometown of North Platte, Nebraska, and gave lavishly to civic groups.[16]

Cody was not only generous with his family and friends but with total strangers as well. When Alexander Majors (formerly of the freighting firm of Russell, Majors, and Waddell) wrote his memoirs, they were printed at Cody's expense and then marketed at *Buffalo Bill's Wild West*. Old scouts did not have to know Cody to receive money. Cody once heard of an old buffalo hunter named William Mathewson in Wichita, Kansas, who was down on his luck and had pawned his buffalo gun. He arranged to have the man's weapon returned to him, and gave Mathewson a retainer for writing his life story without Mathewson knowing the name of his beneficiary.[17]

Children who could not afford *Buffalo Bill's Wild West*, such as orphans, newsboys, and the needy, were often admitted free of charge because Cody loved children. Harry Webb, who worked as a bronc rider in the 1910 season, reported that Cody even had a free performance for blind children because, as Cody put it, he wanted "those kids to at least hear the music and laughter and have the clowns shake hands with them."[18]

In addition to the tens of thousands of children who saw *Buffalo Bill's Wild West* free, Harry Webb stated that Cody would often give free performances at prisons on Sundays. Moreover, in 1906 Cody gave $5,000 to the victims of the Mt. Vesuvius eruption and $1,000 to the victims of the San Francisco earthquake, even though he desperately needed the money for his investments.

Cody's attention to his family was also lavish and costly. After his father Isaac was stabbed, Isaac charged Cody and his older sister, Julia, with taking care of the family. According to Julia, because they knew that their mother Mary was sick and likely to die, they looked for a husband for Julia to help raise the three youngest Cody children, Helen ("Nellie"), Eliza ("Lida"), and Mary ("May"). Subsequently, Julia married Al Goodman on December 22, 1862; about a year later, on November 22, 1863, Mary Cody died.

Before Mary died, she made young Cody promise to take care of his sisters. Cody figured the easiest way to do that was to bring a lawsuit for the value of property sold by an uncle who was cheated. This property amounted to fifty-five acres or $1 million worth of prime real estate in the heart of Cincinnati. Cody's lawyers contended it had been sold by his uncle Phillip Cody when he was not in his right mind. In 1883, Cody reflected on the lawsuit:

The lawyers have great faith in eventually gaining this suit but as it is so very large amounting to so much money and so many and so much money to fight that it takes time and money and with the exception of what little Decker and Faller put up

I have put up every dollar. I have to go security for costs of all the suits besides put up $900.00 cash to day besides all that I have put up if the suit goes against us I will lose all, but have the consolation of carrying out what I promised my poor Mother to do, that is to do all in my power for my sisters.[19]

These lawyers evidently did not do the work because in an 1885 letter Cody gave the case to another lawyer. It is not known how much money Cody spent on this lawsuit, but he pursued it for several years, and his letters refer to money amounting to several thousands. Eventually, Cody apparently dropped the lawsuit.

The Business of Buffalo Bill's Wild West

THE BUSINESS OF RUNNING *BUFFALO BILL'S WILD West* was very complicated. The management teams of *Buffalo Bill's Wild West*, which supported thousands of people who worked for Cody, consisted of Cody, arena manager; Nate Salsbury, business manager; and John M. Burke, front manager and press agent. All of them were superb at their jobs, and the show went smoothly for a decade and a half. It was a huge operation encompassing eleven acres of ground. The arena was 150 feet by 320 feet, and when the exhibition remained in one location for a long time the surface was regulated—drained when wet and sprinkled when dry. During long stays elaborate scenery was used, which was composed of massive painted backdrops with as many as seven panoramas, each 200 feet long and 30 feet high. Although the figures fluctuated due to various factors, such as location, according to Salsbury in an interview during the 1892 London season, to produce *Buffalo Bill's Wild West* it took 22,750 yards of canvas, 20 miles of rope, and 1,104 stakes. Four teams of eighteen men each were assigned specific duties during setup. Since Thomas Edison was a friend of Cody's, it is not surprising that *Buffalo Bill's Wild West* carried with it the largest private electrical plant in existence at the time, capable of powering twenty-four 4,000-candle power

Cody in front of the Deadwood stage. When the riverboat that carried Buffalo Bill's Wild West *collided with another boat on the Mississippi River and sank, one of the few items saved was the Deadwood stage. Courtesy of the Buffalo Bill Historical Center, Cody, Wyoming, Vincent Mercaldo Collection.*

carbon-arc floodlights; one 8,000-candle power searchlight; two 25,000-candle power searchlights; and the house and company lights.[20] Cody was in charge of setup as well as the performances. According to a newspaper account in the Buffalo Bill Historical Center's archives, Cody was adept at both performing in and producing the show:

> *[He] seemed to be omnipresent, sometimes on horseback, sometimes on foot, always unflustered amid the hurrying performers, always ready of eye and hand, with a kind word of advice here or a gentle suggestion there… [he] made all this seemingly chaotic machinery move so well.[21]*

However, despite Cody's skill at managing the performances, sometimes *Buffalo Bill's Wild West* suffered catastrophes, including the sinking of the entire show on the Mississippi River in 1884, numerous train wrecks, lawsuits from strayed bullets, public deaths from runaway animals, performers' deaths in the arena, and a glanders outbreak in France during the 1905 season that necessitated destroying over two hundred horses. Mishaps were so endemic that on June 13, 1896, the official route book of *Buffalo Bill's Wild West* stated:

> *Tonight makes our one hundreth performance this season without missing a show, a railroad accident, or a blow-down. This is remarkable.[22]*

But this luck did not hold. On July 16, a bandwagon did not make it under a bridge during a parade, killing one performer and injuring several others.

Buffalo Bill's Wild West had to keep up with a grueling schedule when the show went on the road. There would be a morning parade followed by two shows; then the crew would pack up the equipment, and the show would travel to the next town. This tight schedule was often complicated by heavy rains that caused wagons to become hopelessly bogged down in mud. The difficult conditions sometimes faced by the show's crew and performers are described by Cody, who wrote the following during the 1908 season:

> *I get soaked to the skin all day nearly everyday… sometimes we are all night getting all our stuff loaded this means late getting to the next town and everybody has to work to get ready to give a performance so its long hours with us.*[23]

Moreover, during the 1898 season, another rainy one, Cody collapsed during a performance in Kansas City. This accounted for two of the nine days he missed during his career in show business, which lasted until he was almost seventy-one years old. Many of Cody's critics claim his absence was caused by drunkenness. After newspapers picked up the story and wrote he was dead, Cody stated:

> *I have just been reading my obituary.… This is what they have happen to me everyday. I was sick for two days in Kansas City, but it was nothing but nervous prostration. The doctors said I had typhoid malarial fever, but that is too stylish for me to have, so I got up and came on about my work.*[24]

The business of a showman was expensive. When *Buffalo Bill's Wild West* was on the road, it cost approximately $4,000 a day to keep it going. To advertise an upcoming show, fliers, posters, and handbills would be circulated. This often led to "circus wars," where competing outfits would fight for billboard space, the price of which would escalate. Such wars were expensive and could bankrupt an outfit. During the Columbian Exposition in Chicago, for example, the cost of billboard space went from between $60 and $70 a week to $300 and $350 a week, and space was often sold twice.[25] This meant that businessmen who had already rented the space had to hire workers to repeatedly post the same bill.

Auburn State Prison, New York. Buffalo Bill's Wild West *often gave free performances in prisons on Sundays. Courtesy of the Buffalo Bill Historical Center, Cody, Wyoming.*

For outfits on the road, routing was a very important factor that helped determine profit and publicity. In 1894, when James A. Bailey became partners with Salsbury and Cody, he took control of the routing and used *Buffalo Bill's Wild West* along with his circuses in his fight with the five Ringling brothers to control the outdoor entertainment world. In 1895, Cody described his involvement in the circus wars in a letter to his brother-in-law Al:

> *You have heard of Circus fights, have you not. Well they are lively affairs—the fighting is done with ink & paper—And I tell you that paper that costs 7 cents a sheet. And newspaper advertisements, and bill boards and brainy men to write, and bill posters to work—costs money. My share of the fight will*

cost me about $15,000. But if we are not making the Ringling Bro. sick you may kick me—No one thought they would have the nerve to give me battle, but they did. And they say they will never do it again. It will cost them at least $60,000. I have downed them in every town they follow me here, and are flooding the city with passes. I am giving out just my regular amount of passes. If my business keeps up the last week, as good as the first, I will leave little money for them to get.[26]

Once Bailey took control of *Buffalo Bill's Wild West*, he wisely routed it in Europe while Bailey's circuses played the United States, shrewdly calculating that there would be more interest in Cody's show in Europe than in the States, as well as less competition.

As the years went by, more and more imitations of *Buffalo Bill's Wild West* appeared and made money riding on Cody's coattails. Most of them used "Wild West" in their names, such as *Buckskin Bill's Wild West, Buffalo and Wild West, Buffalo Tom's Wild West, Indian Bill's Wild West*, and *Lone Bill's Wild West*. Although they were merely cheap imitations of Cody's show, there was enough appeal in the country for such shows to make money even on second-rate presentations. In 1904, one imitation Wild West show even stole Cody's copyrighted name and performed in the same locations. A bogus *Buffalo Bill's Wild West* would arrive in towns before Cody's *Buffalo Bill's Wild West*—using Cody's name, as well as his advertising. As Cody stated, this outfit left "little money for [him] to get."[27] It cost Cody $30,000 in lawyers' fees to stop this practice. Even in Europe Cody occasionally had to battle competition. In 1906, J. T. McCaddon's International Shows, which featured a Wild West show, got into a circus war with *Buffalo Bill's Wild West*. *Buffalo Bill's Wild West* won the war, but the war increased Cody's overhead.

In addition to the Wild West shows, medicine shows also exploited the public's fascination with the West. Indian medicine shows, such as the Kickapoo Medicine Shows, competed for the public's disposable income and sold "medicine" of dubious value. At one time there were over fifty "Kicks," as the trade papers called them, touring North America. Such shows were generally phony and helped to tarnish the image of *Buffalo Bill's Wild West*.

However, the most serious threat to *Buffalo Bill's Wild West* did not come from medicine shows but from two Denver men—Tammen and Bonfils. It was these men who destroyed *Buffalo Bill's Wild West* when Cody imprudently borrowed $20,000 from them at the end of the 1912 season. Harry Tammen and Frederick Bonfils, who owned the *Denver Post*, adhered to the new business morality—as did their contemporaries John D. Rockefeller, Andrew Mellon, and John (J. P.) Pierpont Morgan—that the ends justified the means as long as the ends meant more money for themselves. In his book *Timberline*, Bonfils's and Tammen's biographer Gene Fowler likens these two men to an amorous flea-bitten burro and Alfred Packer, the only man convicted of cannibalism in the United States. They were ruthless and would resort to any tactic to achieve their goals.

Tammen first began accumulating his fortune as a bartender at the Windsor in Denver, where he reportedly stole drink money and then further profited by opening up a museum and curio shop; Bonfils got his money in an illicit lottery. In 1894, the two men then bought the *Denver Post*, using the paper to propagate lies and local scandals. Within ten years it had the largest circulation of any paper in Denver.[28]

Tammen then decided that he wanted to own a circus, stating the rationale for this decision in confusing terms: "[We] were foredamned to success in the circus, as in any other undertaking. What made a circus grow? The truth. A circus is a pack of lies—which is something of a lie itself, because it's only half true, like most paradoxes."[29] Tammen's circus was built on lies from its inception. He purchased a dog and pony show and named it for the *Post*'s sports editor, Otto C. Floto. Because Tammen decided that he needed a "circus" name, he hired a man named William

Cody at a table with a letter, watch, and glasses. Business concerns gradually took control of Cody's life. Courtesy of the Buffalo Bill Historical Center, Cody, Wyoming.

Sells, gave him "a qualifying share or so of stock and thereupon rechristened their show 'The Sells-Floto Circus.'" Thereafter, Tammen billed it as the second largest circus in the world, which was not true.[30]

The Sells-Floto Circus had an unsavory reputation. Ringling Brothers owned the copyright to the Sells Circus name, sued, and the *Post* promptly attacked them as "the Circus Trust" and started another circus war. In addition, the Sells-Floto Circus was poorly managed, and there were instances of animals escaping and killing patrons. In one of these episodes, a tiger escaped and killed a child. Regarding this incident, Tammen's attorney, David C. Webber, argued successfully that since the child was killed after the regular performance and during the tiger's feeding time the circus was not responsible. However, the circus was not so lucky when the elephant "Floto" went on a rampage and killed a church deaconess.

Cody's unfortunate association with Bonfils and Tammen began in 1920. By that time Cody had been business partners with several men: "Doc" Carver, with whom Cody clashed, dissolving their partnership after one year; and Nate Salsbury and James A. Bailey, whom Cody had outlived. After that, when in his mid-sixties, Cody had managed *Buffalo Bill's Wild West* by himself for two years. Then *Buffalo Bill's Wild West* had merged with Pawnee Bill's Show during the 1908 season. By this time Cody was pouring all of the profits from *Buffalo Bill's Wild West* into his Arizona mines and into his town of Cody, Wyoming. Cody's share of the wintering costs for *Buffalo Bill's Wild West* at the end of the 1912 season amounted to $20,000, and he needed to borrow the money. Although Gordon Lillie, a.k.a. Pawnee Bill, had the cash, he refused to loan it to Cody knowing Cody's spendthrift ways. As a result, Cody eventually got the loan, six months at 6 percent, from Tammen.

Cody thought he had signed a promissory note for this loan, but what he actually signed is subject to debate. Cody's copy of the contract dated January 28, 1913, which is at the Buffalo Bill

Historical Center, is not a promissory note but a personal service contract. It is doubtful that Cody or his lawyers ever read it. There is no mention of $20,000 in it, and it contains clauses that Cody would not have agreed to, as well as clauses that Cody could have used to make his services unavailable if he chose to do so. The following lists the points of the contract:

- *Sells-Floto gets an exclusive right to the name "Buffalo Bill";*
- *at the end of the season the profits are to be split at a rate of 60 percent for Sells-Floto, 40 percent for Cody. [Cody was on a 50/50 basis with Lillie];*
- *Cody must give a six-month notice to leave the show before September 1, starting September 1, 1915;*
- *Sells-Floto can use the name "Buffalo Bill" starting immediately;*
- *the contract is binding on heirs;*
- *if Cody is sick, the circus can buy the use of his name;*
- *it was "provided, however, that [Cody] not be required to appear in the saddle or give any performance, except of his own volition."[31]*

By signing this contract, Cody voluntarily demoted himself from being manager of the world's largest outdoor entertainment to being an employee of a two-bit circus.

Once Tammen and Bonfils had Cody's name on the contract, they began to destroy *Buffalo Bill's Wild West*. On February 5, 1913, seven days after the contract was signed, the *Denver Post* announced the following:

The most important deal ever consummated in American amusements enterprises was closed in Denver a few days ago, when Colonel W. F. Cody (Buffalo Bill) put his name to a contract with the proprietors of the Sells-Floto Circus, the gist of which is that these two big shows consolidate for the season of 1914 and thereafter.[32]

When Pawnee Bill read this, he thought his partner Cody had stabbed him in the back. They argued, but soon *Buffalo Bill's Wild West* went on the road. Unfortunately the show was routed through the South during a flood year. Cotton prices were down, and there was a general depression in the entire United States, resulting in poor attendance. The show owners lost a lot of money, and when the company got to Denver they were unable to pay a $60,000 note to the United States Printing and Lithographing Company for printing. Tammen controlled that note, in addition to Cody's $20,000 note, and on July 21, 1914, he sent the sheriff to close *Buffalo Bill's Wild West*. After thirty years on the road, Cody saw his innovative entertainment program put on the auction block; what money he could scrape together he used to pay performers their back wages. By all accounts, seeing *Buffalo Bill's Wild West* auctioned off piece by piece broke Cody's heart. In *Timberline*, Gene Fowler describes the terrible impact Tammen's ruthless actions had on Cody's finances and self-image:

> *To enumerate all the litigations arising from the Cody-Lillie split-up would be endless. Suffice that the hand of the* Post *was felt, if not seen, in much of the court-storm. Bonfils and Tammen had set out to get what they wanted, for little more than the "loss" of their twenty-thousand-dollar loan. They hardly accomplished that aim, for Major Lillie managed to escape with his buckskin pants, his horse, and a few thousand dollars. Not so the gallant Colonel. His creditors realized about fifty cents on the dollar from the sale, but from now on Cody was virtually chattel of the Sells-Floto Circus.*[33]

Ironically, according to later affidavits, Bonfils and Tammen did not even lose the $20,000, though they used it as a lever against Cody for the rest of his life.

The first year Cody toured with the Sells-Floto Circus it must have been agonizing for him. The program from the 1914 tour is filled with pictures of monkeys and articles which must have enraged Cody. For example, the lead article is about the birth of "Elephant Baby Hutch." The warm-up act was Fred Briggs, a female impersonator, and "he'd bring a chuckle to a man with the mumps!" The grand entrance was followed by "Display #2"—Buffalo Bill "Himself." At the time Cody was sixty-eight years old, and after having met the royalty of the world he had been reduced to being part of "a happy family that is formed by the monkeys and orangoutangs in the menagerie of the Sells-Floto Circus and Buffalo Bill (Himself)."[34]

Cody felt that the next tour in 1915 was a disaster waiting to happen; the tents, the ropes, and the crew were rotten. However, according to the files in the Circus World Museum in Baraboo, Wisconsin, the Sells-Floto Circus appears to have been a fine, well-maintained outfit. But regardless of the circus's quality, in Fort Madison, Iowa, there was a flash flood during one of the performances, and most of the crew of four hundred fled, leaving an aging Cody and five crew members to help the women and children to safety. Cody finally became totally disillusioned when he learned that the circus was advertising the cost of the show as twenty-five cents and charging fifty cents at the gate. Tammen and Bonfils were using his name to cheat the American public, and Cody would not stand for that. Consequently, Cody notified them that he would no longer perform. Tammen then traveled to Lawrence, Kansas, to scare Cody by threatening him with a $100,000 lawsuit if Buffalo Bill continued his strike. Cody wrote that he could easily have killed Tammen; when Tammen got to Cody's tent, Tammen became frightened:

> Because he saw danger in the eyes of the old scout, in the gestures of the shaking hand and the guns that hung so near, Tammen wanted to go outside and walk up and down. "I sit right here," said Cody grimly.[35]

To avoid violence, Tammen placated Cody by calling him "father" and lying, leaving Cody with the mistaken belief that everything had been settled in Cody's favor. That was the last year Cody worked for the Sells-Floto Circus.

Cody adapted to these distressing circumstances as he had adapted to other difficult events in his life, such as the stabbing of his father. Cody and Pawnee Bill had once experimented by filming *Buffalo Bill's Wild West* and distributing it but with little success. However, in September 1913 Cody established the film enterprise Colonel W. F. Cody (Buffalo Bill) Historical Pictures Company, the purpose of which was to film battles of the Indian wars with as much realism as possible. The battles were filmed in the actual historical locations with the original combatants—if they were still alive. The result was an epic of eight reels that was so realistic it was horrifying. The reaction of an audience to the "battle" of Wounded Knee was recorded by Hugh O'Neill, a Denver reporter:

As the firing of the carbines ceased and the air cleared we could see the little mounds of dead heaped by the bursting shells on the opposite hillside. Massed together in that way they looked like tents, struck and about to be folded for another march. And each time a shell burst another tent was struck. From a battle between men it had become an afternoon of methodical, wholesale killing. I heard a man praying in whispers... Amen.[36]

This film disappeared shortly after Cody died. Some historians such as William S. E. Coleman and Kevin Browlow would agree with Sarah Emerson Crowley that the government may have been involved in its disappearance:

Whatever its title, the picture has not been seen in any theatre since around 1917; it may have been that Cody's reconstruction of the Wounded Knee was too painfully close to the truth for the U.S. Government.[37]

However, other historians like Paul Fees, senior curator for the Buffalo Bill Historical Center, believe that the most likely

Close friends Frank Powell, Julia Cody, and William Cody on the porch of the Irma Hotel. Courtesy of the Park County Historical Society, Cody, Wyoming.

reason for its disappearance is that it simply was lost. Whatever the truth, the movie failed to make enough profit to pay off the enormous debts Cody had incurred. Because of his financial straits, Cody felt compelled to write to the adjutant general for the $10 a month he thought he was entitled to as a Congressional Medal of Honor recipient.

Soon thereafter, Cody went back on the road, this time with the Miller 101 Ranch show, a company that treated Cody better. He was given a valet to take care of his personal needs, and the company hired Cody's business staff of Johnny Baker and John M. Burke. Because Cody appreciated the respect he was shown by the company, he rode around the arena one time every show, although he was seventy and knew he was dying. Cody's kidneys were failing, and he had rheumatism and arthritis. He wrote his grandson William that "at my age my courage is the one thing that does not fail me."[38]

Shortly after he wrote those words, Cody received a telegram from George Beck, his Cody, Wyoming, manager, that he was bankrupt. The next day Cody wrote a letter about reading the telegram, spending the night thinking about his life, remembering all of his charitable deeds and the people who had lived off Buffalo Bill, and wondering where they were. This is one of the few bitter letters in all of the archives containing Cody material.

The knowledge of the bankruptcy temporarily disabled the dying Cody. During the last two weeks of the Miller 101 Ranch tour, Cody needed to be helped on his horse by Johnny Baker in a curtained alcove. Buffalo Bill would sit there, slumped over in the saddle from pain, until he heard his cue; then the former chief of scouts for the Big Horn Yellowstone Expedition would snap to attention, ride around the arena once, return to the alcove, and collapse. But despite his condition Cody did not miss a single performance during that tour.

Cody went to his sister May's house in Denver to write and consider new schemes to make money. If Cody had been unhampered by the machinations of Tammen and Bonfils, he might have been able to get his finances in order and retire for the last few years of his life. The profits of *Buffalo Bill's Wild West* for the 1912 season were $125,000, and as Cody once said he had "knocked the impossible stiff and cold on more than one occasion."[39] His debts were slightly over $150,000, and one good season's profits could have made him solvent.

While he was staying at his sister's house, Cody's health continued to deteriorate. When Cody's doctor told him he had only a few hours to live, Cody's reaction reflected his stoicism: "Cody roused himself and called for his brother-in-law, Lew Decker, who inquired what the doctor had said. 'Let's forget about it,' said the old scout, 'and play high five.'"[40] Cody died on January 10, 1917. Cody's will of 1906 described in great detail how he wished to be buried:

> *It is my wish and I hereby direct that my body shall be buried in some suitable plot of grooind [sic] on Cedar Mountain, overlooking the town of Cody, Wyoming, in order that my mortal remains shall lie in close proximity to that fair section of my native Country [sic] which bears my name and in the growth and development of which I have taken so deep and loving an interest, and to which wheresoever [sic] and whatever parts of the earth I have wandered I have always longed to return. I further direct that there shall be erected over my grave, to mark the spot where my body lies, a monument wrought from native Red stone in the form of a mammoth Buffalo, and placed in such a position as to be visible from the town, in order that it may be a constant reminder to my fellow citizens that it was the great wish of its founder that Cody should not only grow in prosperity and become a populous and influential metropolis, but that it should be distinguished for the purity of its government and the loyalty of its citizens to the institution of our beloved Country.[41]*

Cody's wish to be buried on Cedar Mountain overlooking Cody, Wyoming, was not honored, however. Instead, Buffalo Bill was buried on Lookout Mountain outside of Denver. The 1906 will left many of Cody's holdings to his daughter Irma and prevented Lulu from receiving anything that she had not already put into her name during Cody's theatrical career. Lulu contested this will, however, presenting a will written in 1913 that left everything to her, which amounted to little since Cody was in debt. Moreover, Lulu stated in *Memories of Buffalo Bill by His Wife* that Cody had requested he be buried on Lookout Mountain so he could look over four states—something that is impossible since the nearest state line is over a 125 miles away. Since it was the *Denver Post* that led the crusade to have Cody buried in Denver, it is more likely that Tammen dragged out the contract he had used so often in the past to bleed Cody and scared Lulu with the "binding on the heirs" clause. A rival newspaper reported conjecture about Tammen's involvement in Cody's burial:

> *It was also said and believed by many people in Denver and Cody that Mrs. Cody was paid ten thousand dollars by Mr. Tammen, for the privilege of selecting, with Bonfils, the burial place... the mortal remains of Buffalo Bill were placed in a vault until the time for the final burial, a time selected by Tammen. This was June 3, 1917. It was a circuslike affair and the Sells-Floto Circus played a part in the parade up the mountain.[42]*

These actions were not out of character for either Lulu or Tammen.

William Cody's Critics

⟨ornament⟩ **ONCE CODY WAS DEAD, HE COULD NO LONGER** reinforce the Buffalo Bill myth. Until late twentieth-century scholars researched the lives and papers of contemporary military leaders like Phillip Sheridan comprehensively, the truth about Cody's heroic career as a scout was unverified and could have been simply attributed to Buffalo Bill's self-serving propaganda. However, even with his credentials as a scout firmly established, in certain areas of his life, Cody's image, inflated by Buffalo Bill fans, could be attacked. His critics could now attack him with impunity, undermining the heroic aspects of the Buffalo Bill myth; Cody himself had provided them with ammunition. This process can be shown in three areas: Buffalo Bill's relationship to Indians, his slaughter of buffalo, and his drinking.

The Yellow Hand incident illustrates the way Cody could be attacked on his relationship with Indians. Cody exploited the factual story and modified it to make it appear more heroic. Harry Webb wrote that while he worked for Cody during the 1910 season, whenever anybody asked how Yellow Hand had died Cody would look at them and reply, "I don't know, old age I guess."[43] Detractors have jumped on this reply to support the statements of other persons present at the Battle of War Bonnet Creek, who claimed to have killed Yellow Hand. They also point to the fact that two seasons after the Yellow Hand fight was presented at Madison Square Garden in 1886 Cody discontinued it in the program of *Buffalo Bill's Wild West*. Cody never stated why he did this, and it could appear that he withdrew that part of the program because he did not kill Yellow Hand and had a guilty conscience. A later statement, however, reveals his motivation may have been to downplay the violence involved. In an interview with the *Denver Post* in 1913, when asked about scalping Yellow Hand Cody replied, "'I regret to say that I did. I was carried away by the thought of Custer. I jerked off Yellow Hand's big bonnet, grasped his war-lock and cut it off.' The interviewer asked if that wasn't a bloodthirsty thing to do, 'Yes,' said the Colonel, 'And that is why I seldom refer to the duel.'"[44]

To make Cody's relationship to Indians appear suspect, Cody's critics also quote Indian agents and religious leaders who accused him of exploiting the first Americans. However, such accusations on the part of Indian agents and religious leaders occurred because Cody was interested in helping Indians preserve their culture, while the government and church wanted to assimilate Indians into white culture, making them conform to Euro-American standards. Over the objections of the "reformers" who wanted to see the Indian's culture obliterated, Cody had them present the Ghost Dance, the Sun Dance, the War Dance, the Corn Dance, and other ethnic celebrations that reinforced the Indian's culture.

Moreover, it is clear that Cody spoke for understanding between the two races from the beginning of his stage career. Cody was often a speaker at civic functions, and the following excerpt from Cody's speech at the John Wanamaker dinner, a fundraiser for a sculpture the size of the Statue of Liberty of an Indian welcoming immigrants to America, reflects his respect for Indians:

I have known the redman ... since I was a baby. I have known him on the warpath and in peace, and I have known him to be always honorable in peace or war.

He has been driven back and forth over the country of which he once was lord. They ask me why the Indian is cruel and why he has so frequently gone to war with the white man, and all I can say is that I do not know. But I can quote old Sitting Bull, that great Indian chief, who said: "I have seen the bones of white men on the Indian's land, but never have I seen the bones of Indians on white men's land."

The Indian welcomed the Pilgrim father and was glad to give him land and call him brother. Then more white men came and they crowded the Indian back over the Alleghenies and then over the Mississippi and then over the Missouri until to-day he has only the reservations to live upon. They drove the Indian to land that was thought only to be good for the rattlesnake and the coyote, and he couldn't even stay there when the white man found that his land was useful.

I have served under thirty-two different generals as scout and guide, and I never pointed a gun at an Indian, that I did not feel in my heart a profound and sincere regret.[45]

Another indication of Cody's respect for Indians was his decent treatment of the Indians he employed. For example, when Cody was filming his movie about the Indian wars in 1913, not only did he pay the Indians $5 a day and treat them to a merry-go-round (the Indians of *Buffalo Bill's Wild West* had enjoyed merry-go-rounds during the Columbian Exposition twenty years previously), but at the end of the film's shooting Cody paid them, out of his own pocket, $1,313 due to them in back wages from the time when *Buffalo Bill's Wild West* had folded in Denver. Even though Cody himself was struggling financially at the time, his word was his bond; the Indians knew and respected this.[46]

Further, during the 1885 season of *Buffalo Bill's Wild West*, Cody gave Sitting Bull a generous contract. Sitting Bull also insisted that the money made from the sale of his photographs and autographs, which was considerable, go to him. Sitting Bull, in turn, sent money home to his Sioux people or gave it to the needy children who would follow the company members around. The only thing that Sitting Bull ever bought for himself was hard candy and oyster stew, which he loved. Sitting Bull used to say that he could not understand how the white man could let children starve in a land of plenty.

The Indian's trust of Cody is illustrated by an incident that occurred prior to the filming of the reenactment of the Wounded Knee massacre. The old Sioux leaders came to tell Cody that some of the young men had procured live ammunition and were going to attack General Miles and the troops during the reenactment. In a midnight conference, Cody talked them out of it; he was one of the few white men who could influence the Indians, and because of his actions many lives were saved.

The irony that Cody saved lives in this instance can only be appreciated by reviewing the circumstances of the winter 1890 massacre at Wounded Knee. At that time General Miles had asked Cody to go to that area and bring in Sitting Bull for questioning concerning the Ghost Dance disturbance. Practitioners of the Ghost Dance felt that the white man had rejected their God by crucifying him, and that if they danced hard enough God would reward them by restoring the bison herds, as well as their dead relatives. At the time, many authority figures incorrectly believed that the great Lakota mystic Sitting Bull was behind the Ghost Dance craze. Miles knew Cody and Sitting Bull respected each other and had become friends while Sitting Bull had worked for Cody during the 1885 season of *Buffalo Bill's Wild West*. Although Cody and his "blood brother" Dr. Franklin (White Beaver) Powell went, Cody's mission was thwarted by the Indian agent, Major John McLaughlin, who only knew Buffalo Bill and White Beaver from dime novels and thought this mission was a publicity stunt. After Cody was relieved of his mission, McLaughlin sent out the Indian police to bring Sitting Bull in, who resisted and was killed. The Unkpapa, Sitting Bull's tribe, thought they were going to be massacred so they fled the reservation to Big Foot's people along Wounded Knee Creek, where the Seventh Cavalry caught up with them. The Sioux were surrendering their weapons when somebody fired a shot, and more than 150 Indians, mostly unarmed, were slaughtered by the Seventh Cavalry. Ironically, although Buffalo Bill was not able to save Indian lives in 1890 because of a white man's meddling, Cody did save lives in 1913 because of cooperation with Indians.

A final point about Cody's attitude toward Indians that has been overlooked by all of his chroniclers is that his best friend Dr. Powell was part Indian and a notorious Populist politician who faced racism his entire political life. Powell spent a lot of his time with Cody and *Buffalo Bill's Wild West*, not only to be with his "blood brother," but undoubtedly also to associate with Indian people and others who were not prejudiced about his race.

A second focus of criticism of Cody is his alleged annihilation of buffalo herds. While some historians have accused Cody of single-handedly annihilating the buffalo herds, other historians argue that he did not hunt buffalo at all, but made up hunting stories while consuming large quantities of whiskey.[47] Cody's skill as a hunter has been too thoroughly documented to argue that he never hunted buffalo, but how many he killed and what effect this had on the buffalo population is open to discussion. From October 1867 to May 1868, while Cody was hunting for the Goddard brothers supplying the Kansas Pacific Railroad with buffalo meat, he killed 4,280 buffalo. But this was the only time he was employed as a meat hunter. The other hunting parties he led were of shorter duration, and often the people he was guiding were interested in other game animals. The meat from these hunts went to military outposts that furnished the escort; in this way the post could rationalize the expenditure for a guide.

Estimates of the buffalo population when Cody started hunting vary, but if we assume a conservative figure of 10 million bison, and if Cody was responsible for the death of 10,000 animals (a high figure), then Cody killed only .001 percent of the

William Cody and Louisa Cody on a train platform. Despite all their disagreements and troubles, William and Louisa stayed together. Courtesy of the Buffalo Bill Historical Center, Cody, Wyoming.

buffalo herds. It is clear that the near extermination of the buffalo came from other sources.

The railroads were a major cause of extermination. They continually cut the herds' grazing territory and also advertised for "sportsmen" to ride the trains and shoot out the windows to satisfy their pernicious need to kill. Unfortunately, these sportsmen rarely killed the animals but only wounded them.

Perhaps the deadliest foe of the buffalo were hide hunters. Hide hunters such as Jim White could scoff at the estimated 10,000 buffalo Cody had killed when White could claim as many kills in two years.[48] Many of these hide hunters felt that the buffalo supply was endless; in addition, their activities were encouraged by the military, which wanted the buffalo herds eliminated to force the Indians onto the reservations. Cody correctly summed up the shortsightedness and cruelty of the hide hunters in an article entitled "The Buffalo: Who Has Slain Them by Tens of Thousands?":

> *The number of animals killed by me and by other white men and all the tribes of Indians, for food, would seem enormous if it could be correctly written down, yet all that killing, so long as it was confined to such legitimate supply, did not seriously diminish the herds...the death knell of the buffaloes sounded when white men got to killing them for their hides, simply to make leather. For that use they could kill at any season of the year, and they did, cruelly, recklessly—exterminating them for the sake of the two or four dollars each they got for the hides, and leaving the carcasses by the hundreds of thousands to rot on the plains.*[49]

By exhibiting buffalo in *Buffalo Bill's Wild West*, Cody helped focus the world's attention on the fact that buffalo were rapidly becoming extinct. Newspapers such as England's *Birmingham Gazette* noted that "additional interest is attached to the buffaloes by the fact that they are almost an extinct species."[50] This type of observation by newspaper reporters often preceded the presentation of *Buffalo Bill's Wild West* in many locations and made the world aware that something needed to be done if the buffalo was to be saved from extinction.

A third type of criticism often heard about Cody involves his drinking. It has frequently been said that Cody was just an old wineskin, a drunk who told a good story and sat a good horse. Ironically, many stories about Cody's excessive drinking originated with Cody himself, who enjoyed building up his reputation as a big drinker. Even though Cody did have an enormous capacity for alcohol, he was also aware of embellishing drinking episodes for entertainment. As he said concerning a story he was writing:

"I have got to put in a lot of drunks to liven the book. Who ever heard of anything funny without booze."[51]

Although Cody died of uremic poisoning, often associated with chronic drinking, his work record shows that drinking did not interfere with his job. Nate Salsbury constantly worried about his partner's predilection to drink and got Cody to promise to remain sober while *Buffalo Bill's Wild West* was touring. Press clippings from England during Queen Victoria's Golden Jubilee in 1887 remark on Cody's abstinence and the English Salvation Army's desire to have him speak on the topic of sobriety. When not touring, however, Cody did drink considerably. His drinking bouts in North Platte, Nebraska, and Cody, Wyoming, are legendary. What is often overlooked is that, according to William McDonald, Cody at least tried to stop drinking around 1908:

> *William McDonald stated often that Cody entirely left off drinking alcoholic beverages during the last nine years of his life. When he "set 'em up" for others after his sixty-fourth year, or was offered a drink himself, he always took lemonade, McDonald said. The Colonel's abstinence was due, in part, to his doctor's orders, but Mrs. Cody may have had much to do with it.[52]*

This is supported by a New York reporter, who went on a hunt with Cody and was amazed that there was no drinking because Cody's friends deferred to Cody's abstinence.[53] The George Beck file at the American Heritage Center in Laramie, Wyoming, also reveals a man struggling to stop drinking.

Critics of Cody tend to focus on his unhealthy drinking habits because this weakness makes Cody an easy target. However, such critics fail to view Cody's drinking in historical context. Instead, it is necessary to keep in mind that Cody was a man raised on the Plains with men who drank to relieve the boredom of a hot, monotonous job and the stress of living in a hostile environment. From the age of eleven Cody was working a man's job with tough men, and by his own account he started drinking around the age of fourteen. Cody and his business partner, "Doc" Carver, both drank a lot during the 1883 season of *Buffalo Bill's Wild West*. Although the show was sloppy, there is no record of Cody missing a performance because of drunkenness as Carver did. Once Nate Salsbury took over the business management of *Buffalo Bill's Wild West* Cody stayed sober during tours and refused to tolerate drinking among his employees.

In summary, of the criticisms leveled at Cody—that he wasn't a scout, exploited the Indians, exterminated the buffalo, and was a drunkard, this last charge is the only one that is not totally spurious.

The Decline of Wild West Shows

By the time America entered World War I, there were no longer any Wild West shows on the road. Occasionally, one has toured since that time, usually unsuccessfully. The Sandusky, Ohio, *Daily Journal and Local News* clearly stated the reason why Wild West shows eventually disappeared: "In another generation such an exhibition will be an impossibility. It is given by men who are to the manor born, and they can never be replaced."[54]

By the end of Cody's career, the image of Buffalo Bill had become less idealistic: he was an old man; his highly publicized divorce hearing had revealed an unflattering side of his character; his "Final Farewell Tours" had become a joke with the press; and the publicity that surrounded Cody's oft-proclaimed desire to serve as a scout during the 1898 Spanish-American War backfired because by that time Buffalo Bill was too enmeshed in his businesses to serve in the war.

In addition, Cody had to face great societal changes in his final years as Richard Hofstadter explains:

> *For a generation after the Civil War, a time of great economic exploitation and waste, a [time of] grave social corruption and*

*ugliness, the dominant note in American political life was
complacency. Although dissenting minorities were always
present, they were submerged by the overwhelming realities of
industrial growth and continental settlement.*[55]

Starting in the 1880s, the Populist movement helped to
release the pent-up anger and desire for reform in the American
public. At the turn of the century, labor movements, professional
groups, and social workers like Jane Addams and Jacob Riis were
solidifying their power and looking towards the future, not the
past, as personified by Buffalo Bill. Even Cody's "blood brother"
White Beaver Powell, who headed the most egalitarian and radi-
cal platform in the country when he ran for governor of
Wisconsin, could not successfully weather the racially divisive
stormy times.

The show business world underwent enormous change as
entertainment branched out into rodeos and homespun versions
of many of the Wild West acts. Cody's audiences also became
more sophisticated, while movies added new competition.
Although Cody realized the potential of movies, his version of the
Wild West did not translate well to film due to the fact that
Buffalo Bill's Wild West was based on the physical presence of Wild
West characters and animals. In addition, the automobile also
gained popularity, and family drives became a form of entertainment as well, draining income from other types of entertainment.

The very mythic nature of the Wild West also undermined the
business of Wild West shows because the modern public, con-
cerned with the realities of industrial growth, could no longer
relate as well to the Wild West experience. Although Buffalo Bill
had been an institution, Cody was reduced to playing one-night
stands and cashing in on name recognition. However, because of
all of the cheap imitations of Buffalo Bill on the market, in his
final years Cody had to be billed as "Buffalo Bill, Himself." In
addition, writers like Horatio Alger began to change the image of
children, making it appear that they were incapable of performing

feats of physical heroism such as Cody had performed in his youth. According to Alger, children got ahead by using their brains. Child labor laws also changed the view of children. In the real world there were now laws protecting children from being abused, and according to this new perspective Cody's childhood could be seen as abusive and unrealistic.

Moreover, the horrors of the Indian wars of the 1850s were foreign to the public of the 1900s, which was increasingly urban and predominately composed of immigrants or first-generation Americans. The United States was rapidly becoming a country of conformists, and a rugged individualist like Cody became an undesirable anachronism. Today, however, many people have nostalgia for the type of individual Buffalo Bill Cody personified. Annie Oakley best summed up Buffalo Bill's qualities in the following eulogy:

He was the kindest, simplest, most loyal man I ever knew. He was the staunchest friend. He was in fact the personification of those sturdy and lovable qualities that really made the West, and they were the final criterion of all men, East and West. Like all really great and gentle men he was not a fighter by preference. His relations with everyone he came in contact with were the most cordial and trusting of any man I ever knew....

It may seem strange that after the wonderful success attained, he should have died a poor man. But it isn't a matter of wonder to those who knew him and worked with him. The same qualities that insured success also insured his ultimate poverty. His generosity and kind-hearted attitude toward all comers, his sympathy and his broad understanding of human nature, made it the simplest thing possible to handle men, both in his show and throughout the world. But by the same token he was totally unable to resist any claim for assistance that came to him, or refuse any mortal in distress. His philosophy was that of the plains and the camp, more nearly Christian and charitable than we are used to finding in the sharp business world he was encountering for the first time. The pity of it was that not only could anyone that wanted a loan or a gift get it for the asking, but he never seemed to lose his trust in the nature of all men, and until his dying day he was the easiest mark above ground for every kind of sneak and goldbrick vendor that was mean enough to take advantage of him.

I never saw him in any situation that changed his natural attitude a scintilla. None could possibly tell the difference between his reception of a band of cowboys or the train of an emperor....

His heart never left the great West. Whenever the day's work was done, he could always be found sitting alone watching the sinking sun, and at every opportunity he took the trail back to his home. The sun setting over the mountain will pay its daily tribute to the resting place of the last of the great builders of the West.[56]

In conclusion, no matter how Cody is judged, *Buffalo Bill's Wild West* mesmerized audiences for thirty years, dominating show business of Cody's era. As Paul Fees wrote:

Whatever aspect of the Wild West shows is considered, the subject matter inevitably comes back to Buffalo Bill. He started the Wild West show and he dominated it; only sporadically did it survive him. The public came as much to see Buffalo Bill as they did to see his show; he was the dime novel hero come to life, and they cared little that he was also authentically the scout and plainsman he was advertised to be. All other shows were imitative, however much they claimed to be the real Wild West or the historic Wild West.[57]

Notes

Introduction

1. Gene Fowler, *Timberline: A Story of Bonfils and Tammen* (New York: Garden City Publishing Company, 1933), 312.

2. Luther (Lute) North was the brother of Major Frank North; he argued that his brother should have received the fame and fortune Cody found. After Cody died and as North got older, he became more extravagant in his claims. See Luther North, *A Man of the Plains: Recollections of Luther North* (Lincoln: University of Nebraska Press, 1961). James William Buel wrote a glowing and often inaccurate account of Cody's life. See James William Buel, *Heroes of the Plains* (San Francisco, Calif.: A. L. Bancroft & Co., 1883).

3. Don Russell, *The Lives and Legends of Buffalo Bill* (Norman: University of Oklahoma Press, 1960). No doubt Russell would have made these revisions if he had had the appropriate information, because his was a continuing scholarship as is shown in the University of Nebraska's new edition of *The Life of the Hon. William F. Cody Known as Buffalo Bill*, edited by Don Russell, where Russell verifies, with a newly discovered newspaper clipping, the story of Isaac Cody's stabbing over the slavery issue through a direct citation Russell could not make in his previously published *The Lives and Legends of Buffalo Bill*.

4. Salsbury Collection, Bieneke Library, Yale University, New Haven, Connecticut.

Part 1

The Buffalo Bill Historical Center is identified by B.B.H.C. and the appropriate files.

1. Gene Fowler, *Timberline: A Story of Bonfils and Tammen* (New York: Garden City Publishing Company, 1933), 272.

2. Henry Nash Smith, *Virgin Land* (Cambridge, Mass.: Harvard University Press, 1950), vii.

3. Richard Slotkin, "The Wild West," in *Buffalo Bill and the Wild West* (New York: Brooklyn Museum, 1981), 28.

4. Don Russell, ed., "Julia Cody Goodman's Memoirs of Buffalo Bill," *Kansas Historical Quarterly* 28, no. 4 (Winter 1962): 480.

5. Don Russell, *The Lives and Legends of Buffalo Bill* (Norman: University of Oklahoma Press, 1960), 50. "Pony" Bob Haslam made the longest ride of

380 miles during the Paiute War in Nevada, and Howard Egan made a ride of 330 miles. Although Cody's sister Helen claimed in a book that Cody's ride was the longest in history, her assertion was incorrect—aimed at publicity.

6. After one of my lectures at the Buffalo Bill Historical Center, I was informed by a librarian from Hays, Kansas, that there is a monument to Rome, Kansas, and a sign on the railroad's route marking it.

7. Ellis County Historical Society, *Homesteader* (February 1975): 1.

8. The 1885 *Buffalo Bill's Wild West* program, 5.

9. B.B.H.C., 1914 scrapbook, 20.

10. William Frederick Cody, *The Life of the Hon. William F. Cody Known as Buffalo Bill* (Lincoln: University of Nebraska Press, 1978), 263.

11. These stories did not appear in a book until 1881, long after Cody's association with Buntline had ended.

12. Cody, *The Life*, 282.

13. Henry Eugene Davies, *Ten Days on the Plains* (New York: Crocker & Co., 1871), 29.

14. Cody, *The Life*, 289–90.

15. B.B.H.C., 1909–1910 scrapbook, 6.

16. Robert M. Utley, *Frontier Regulars* (Lincoln: University of Nebraska Press, 1973), 8.

17. Paul Hutton, "From Little Bighorn to Little Big Man: The Changing Image of a Western Hero in Popular Culture," *The Western Historical Quarterly* 7 (January 1976).

18. Cody, *The Life*, 311.

19. B.B.H.C., 1875–1880 scrapbook.

20. James L. Roark, *Masters without Slaves* (New York: W. W. Norton & Co., 1977), 120.

21. William Gienappe, lecture notes, April 1986.

22. Robert H. Wiebe, *The Search for Order 1877–1920* (New York: Hill and Wang, 1967), 5.

23. Ibid., 66.

24. Russell Nye, *The Unembarrassed Muse: The Popular Arts in America* (New York: Dial Press, 1970), 201.

25. Albert Johannsen, *The House of Beadle and Adams and Its Dime and Nickel Novels*, vol. 1 (Norman: University of Oklahoma Press, 1950), 39, quoting the *Banner Weekly* 8, no. 368, November 3, 1889.

26. Ibid., 3–4.

27. John Fraser, *America and the Patterns of Chivalry* (London, England: Cambridge University Press, 1982), 9.

28. Ibid., 66.

29. B.B.H.C., 1909–1910 scrapbook, 2.

30. *Ellis County* (Kansas) *Star*, June 29, 1876.

31. Russell, *Lives*, 22.

32. Cody, *The Life*, 355–56.

33. Ibid., 360.

34. Mark Siegel, *American Culture and the Classic Western Movie* (Japan: Eihosha, L.T.D., 1984), 34.

35. Philip I. Mitterling, "Buffalo Bill and Carry Nation: Symbols of an Age," *North Dakota Quarterly* 50 (Winter 1982): 60–69.

36. *Ledger Company "C,"* 11.

37. Ibid., 134–35.

38. *Mark Twain's Scrap Book*, 13.

39. Ibid., 22.

40. Ibid., 23.

41. Russell, *Lives*, 413.

42. Johannsen, *The House of Beadle and Adams*, vol. 2, 60.

43. Cody, *The Life*, xviii.

44. Cody, *The Life*, 41.

45. Elizabeth Jane Leonard and Julia Cody Goodman, *Buffalo Bill: King of the Old West* (New York: Library Publishers, 1955), 87: "Under Hickok's tutelage, Billy soon was a crack shot. But Billy learned something much more important than marksmanship from Wild Bill; imitating his mentor in every respect he inadvertently became a gentleman." This is one of my reasons to suppose a brotherly relationship between the two men, but there are many: Cody's brother, Stephen, was five years older than Cody when Stephen died; Hickok was nine years older. Cody and Hickok had many similar tastes in clothes and hairstyles; they both were extremely fond of children, women, and horses. Even though Cody stayed on the stage for over a decade, both he and Hickok felt extremely foolish acting; the only difference was that Cody used it as a "means to an end" as his sister Helen states in her book. According to Leonard and Goodman (*King*, 100–01), Hickok proposed to Julia, and Cody told her not to do it because "he [Hickok] loves the plains, he lives for adventure, and even though he'd try with all his might, he could never settle down." (This quote about Hickok could also apply to Cody after he married Louisa.) In spite of being rejected by Julia, Hickok was an honored guest of the Cody household

even when Cody wasn't there. Hickok frequently lived there, and his letters to his family in Illinois are often from Cody's home. The work of Leonard and Goodman shows a lot of "art" on Leonard's part and is embellished from "Julia Cody Goodman's Memoirs of Buffalo Bill," *Kansas Historical Quarterly* 28, no. 4 (Winter 1962). However, there is a basis of truth in *King*. One final note: Cody never depicted a gunfight in *Buffalo Bill's Wild West*, although he exploited every other kind of western scenario. Hickok was one of the finest gunfighters of the Old West, and perhaps this topic brought too many painful memories to Cody about his friend Wild Bill.

46. Cody, *The Life*, 135.

47. Paul Fees, "Unregimented Heroes: Civilian Scouts in the Indian Wars," Paper given on October 19, 1984, at the Western Historical Association, St. Paul, Minnesota, 7.

48. James William Buel, *Heroes of the Plains* (San Francisco, Calif.: A. L. Bancroft & Co., 1883), 322.

49. Buel, *Heroes*, 339–44.

50. Russell, *Lives*, 274–75.

51. Helen Cody Wetmore, *Last of the Great Scouts: The Life Story of Col. William F. Cody as Told by His Sister* (Chicago: Duluth Press Publishing Company, 1899), 3.

52. Kent Ladd Steckmesser, *The Western Hero in History and Legend* (Norman: University of Oklahoma Press, 1965).

53. Wetmore, *Last*, 31. Although the wording is slightly different, this pledge also shows up in the histories of Leonard and Goodman, *King*, 75; Richard J. Walsh, *The Making of Buffalo Bill: A Study in Heroics* (Indianapolis, Ind.: Bobbs-Merrill Company, 1928, 42; and Buel, *Heroes*, 247.

54. Wetmore, *Last*, 84.

55. Richard J. Walsh and Milton S. Salsbury, *The Making of Buffalo Bill* (Kissimmee, Fla.: Cody Publications, 1978), 17; Russell, *Lives*, 203; Henry Blackman Sell and Victor Weybright, *Buffalo Bill and the Wild West* (New York: Signet Key Books, 1959), 128–130.

56. Sarah J. Blackstone, *Buckskins, Bullets, and Business: A History of Buffalo Bill's Wild West* (New York: Greenwood Press, 1986), 50–51. Also see: Charles Phillip Fox and Tom Parkinson, *Billers, Banners, and Bombast: The Story of Circus Advertising* (Boulder, Colo.: Pruett Publishing Company, 1985), 7, 11–12.

57. London *Globe*, 1887.

58. *The Chicago Herald*, April 23, 1893.

59. Paul Fees, lecture to Herman Viola's summer institute class, B.B.H.C., summer 1986.

60. B.B.H.C., 1883–1888 scrapbook.

61. The 1885 *Buffalo Bill's Wild West* program.

62. *The Daily Item* (Troy, New York), June 8, 1898.

63. *Eve' News* (London, England), August 13, 1892.

64. Kathy Peiss, *Cheap Amusements* (Philadelphia: Temple University Press, 1986), 140.

65. B.B.H.C., 1892 scrapbook, 128.

66. Ibid., 134.

67. Louisa Frederici Cody, *Memories of Buffalo Bill by His Wife* (New York: D. Appleton & Co., 1919), 255–56.

68. Blackstone, *Buckskins, Bullets*, 64.

69. Cody, *Memories*, 249–50.

70. Luther North, *A Man of the Plains: Recollections of Luther North* (Lincoln: University of Nebraska Press, 1961), 150.

71. Vine Deloria, Jr., "The Indians," in *Buffalo Bill and the Wild West* (New York: Brooklyn Museum, 1981). Deloria is very complimentary about Cody's enlightened treatment of the Indians and cites many of Cody's statements about the Indian, such as "'In nine cases out of ten when there is trouble between white men and Indians, it will be found that the white man is responsible. Indians expect a man to keep his word. They can't understand how a man can lie. Most of them would as soon cut off a leg as tell a lie'" (51).

72. *The Stamford* (Connecticut) *Telegram*, May 24, 1898.

Part 2

1. Nellie Snyder Yost, *Buffalo Bill* (Chicago: The Swallow Press, 1979), 162.

2. *The La Crosse* (Wisconsin) *Morning Chronicle*, December 4, 1890.

3. Yost, *Buffalo Bill*, 316–17.

4. Stella Adelyne Foote, *Letters from Buffalo Bill* (Billings, Mont.: Foote Publishing Company, 1954).

5. Louisa Frederici Cody, *Memories of Buffalo Bill by His Wife* (New York: D. Appleton & Co., 1919), 30.

6. B.B.H.C., 1909–1910 scrapbook, 9, newspaper unidentified.

7. From Elizabeth Lambert Wood's "Arizona Hoof Trails," *Oracle Historian* (Summer 1980): 6.

8. B.B.H.C., 1909–1910 scrapbook, 20, newspaper unidentified.

9. For information about the Copper Giant, see Eric V. Sorg, "The

Skinning of White Beaver Powell," in *Old West* (Stillwater, Okla.: Western Publications, 1993).

10. B.B.H.C., letter to George Hinkle, May 14, 1902.

11. Charles A. Welch, *History of the Big Horn Basin* (Salt Lake City, Utah: Deseret News Press, 1940), 60.

12. B.B.H.C., letter to George Hinkle, June 4, 1901.

13. Richard J. Walsh, *The Making of Buffalo Bill: A Study in Heroics* (Indianapolis, Ind.: Bobbs-Merrill Company, 1928), 322–23.

14. Ibid.

15. *Letters*, 47–48. This and the following Cody letters are often grammatically incorrect with words frequently misspelled. Although his letters became more sophisticated as he got older, Cody had a very limited education and was a self-made man. Despite this lack of formal education, Cody had a sharp intellect and knew and conversed in a sophisticated manner with the elite of the late nineteenth century.

16. Yost, *Buffalo Bill*, 250–51. Yost's book often reads like a gossip column. It is a collection of stories that circulated around North Platte.

17. Don Russell, *The Lives and Legends of Buffalo Bill* (Norman: University of Oklahoma Press, 1960), 92. This story was confirmed by the Wichita Historical Museum in 1982.

18. B.B.H.C., Harry Webb, vertical file, "Buffalo Bill Saint or Devil," 12.

19. Foote, *Letters*, 23.

20. Sarah J. Blackstone, *Buckskins, Bullets, and Business: A History of Buffalo Bill's Wild West* (New York: Greenwood Press, 1986), 45–46.

21. B.B.H.C., 1898 scrapbook, "E," newspaper unidentified.

22. 1896 route book of *Buffalo Bill's Wild West*.

23. B.B.H.C., MS 6, box 1, folder 20.

24. B.B.H.C., 1898 scrapbook, 130.

25. B.B.H.C., 1893 scrapbook, 30.

26. Foote, *Letters*, 43.

27. Lucille Nichols Patrick, *The Best Little Town by a Dam Site or Cody's First 20 Years* (Cheyenne, Wyo.: Flintlock Publishing Co., 1968), 83.

28. Gene Fowler, *Timberline: A Story of Bonfils and Tammen* (New York: Garden City Publishing Company, 1933), 46–48.

29. Ibid., 209.

30. Ibid., 207–09.

31. B.B.H.C., oversize box 5.

32. *Denver Post*, February 5, 1913.

33. Fowler, *Timberline*, 380.

34. The 1914 Sells-Floto Circus program, 1–6.

35. Walsh, *The Making*, 353.

36. Hugh O'Neill, *Denver Post*; B.B.H.C., 1914 scapbook, 31.

37. Sarah Emmerson Crowley, *Tombstone Epitaph*, June 1980, 9.

38. B.B.H.C., MS6 Series 2B.

39. Paul Fees, Ephemeral file.

40. Henry Blackman Sell and Victor Weybright, *Buffalo Bill and the Wild West* (New York: Signet Key Books, 1959), 297.

41. B.B.H.C., oversize Box 5.

42. Sell and Weybright, *Buffalo Bill*, 298–99.

43. B.B.H.C., Harry Webb vertical file.

44. Fowler, *Timberline*, 375.

45. B.B.H.C., 1909–1910 scrapbook, 12.

46. Crowley, *Tombstone Epitaph*, 8.

47. See Mari Sandoz's *The Buffalo Hunters* (New York: Hastings House, 1954) for his rendition of Cody's buffalo hunting days. Sandoz paints a portrait of a man whose only ability was drinking whiskey and collecting a paycheck on other men's work. Sandoz's methodology and documentation are questionable.

48. End of Trail Museum, Cody, Wyoming.

49. Paul Fees's files, *New York Journal*, May 16, 1897.

50. *Birmingham* (England) *Gazette*, November 4, 1887.

51. B.B.H.C., MS 6, box 1, folder 25.

52. Yost, *Buffalo Bill*, 365.

53. Don Russell, *The Wild West*(Fort Worth, Tex.: Amon Carter Museum of Western Arts, 1970), 105.

54. Sandusky, Ohio, *Daily Journal and Local News*, July 12, 1898.

55. Richard Hofstadter, *The Age of Reform* (New York: Vintage Books, 1960), 60.

56. Isabelle S. Sayers, *Annie Oakley and Buffalo Bill's Wild West* (New York: Dover Publications, 1981), 83–85.

57. Paul Fees, Ephemeral file.

Bibliography

Books and Articles

Blackstone, Sarah J. *Buckskins, Bullets, and Business: A History of Buffalo Bill's Wild West*. New York: Greenwood Press, 1986.

Bowles, Samuel. *Our New West*. Hartford, Conn.: Hartford Publishing Company, 1869.

Buel, James William. *Heroes of the Plains*. San Francisco, Calif.: A. L. Bancroft & Co., 1883.

Buntline, Ned (Edward Zane Carroll Judson). *Buffalo Bill: The King of the Border Men*. Edited by William Roba. Davenport, Ia.: Service Press, 1987. Periodical serial, December 23, 1869, to March 3, 1870.

Burke, John. *Buffalo Bill: The Noblest Whiteskin*. New York: G. P. Putnam's Sons, 1973.

Burke, John M. *Buffalo Bill from Prairie to Palace*. Chicago: Rand McNally & Co., 1893.

Cawelti, John G. *The Six-gun Mystique*. Bowling Green, N.Y.: Bowling Green University Popular Press, 1971.

Cody, Louisa Frederici. *Memories of Buffalo Bill by His Wife*. New York: D. Appleton & Co., 1919.

Cody, William Frederick. *The Life of the Hon. William F. Cody Known as Buffalo Bill*. Hartford, Conn.: Frank E. Bliss, 1879; reprint Lincoln: University of Nebraska Press, 1978.

___. *Story of the Wild West and Campfire Chats, by Buffalo Bill (Hon. W. F. Cody): A Full and Complete History of the Renowned Pioneer Quartette, Boone, Crockett, Carson and Buffalo Bill*. Chicago: Stanton and Van Vliet Co., 1901.

___. *White Beaver's Still Hunt; or The Miner Marauder's Death Track*. New York: Beadle & Adams, 1894.

___. *The Wizard Brothers; or White Beaver's Red Trail*. New York: Beadle & Adams, 1886.

Connelley, William Elsey. *Wild Bill and His Era*. New York: The Press of the Pioneers, 1933.

Cooper, Jerry M. "The Wisconsin National Guard in the Milwaukee Riots of 1886." *Wisconsin Magazine of History* 55, no. 1 (Autumn 1971).

Daley, W. W. *Lost Towns of Carbon County*. Cheyenne, Wyo.: Works Progress Administration, subject 860.

Davies, Henry Eugene. *Ten Days on the Plains*. New York: Crocker & Co., 1871.

Deahl, William Evans, Jr. "A History of Buffalo Bill's Wild West Show." Diss., Southern Illinois University, 1974.

Deloria, Vine, Jr. "The Indians." In *Buffalo Bill and the Wild West*. New York: Brooklyn Museum, 1981.

Dextor, William Fellows, and Andrew A. Freeman. *This Way to the Big Show*. New York: Viking Press, 1936.

Fees, Paul. "Unregimented Heroes: Civilian Scouts in the Indian Wars." Paper given on October 19, 1984, at the Western Historical Association, St. Paul, Minnesota.

Fisher, John R. "The Royal and Duncan Pursuits: Aftermath of the Battle of Summit Springs." *Nebraska History* 50, no. 3 (Fall 1969).

Foote, Stella Adelyne. *Letters from Buffalo Bill*. Billings, Mont.: Foote Publishing Company, 1954.

Fowler, Gene. *Timberline: A Story of Bonfils and Tammen*. New York: Garden City Publishing Company, 1933.

Fox, Charles Phillip, and Tom Parkinson. *Billers, Banners, and Bombast: The Story of Circus Advertising*. Boulder, Colo.: Pruett Publishing Company, 1985.

Fraser, John. *America and the Patterns of Chivalry*. London, England: Cambridge University Press, 1982.

Grinnell, George Bird. *The Fighting Cheyennes*. Norman: University of Oklahoma Press, 1956.

___. *Two Great Scouts and Their Pawnee Battalion*. Cleveland, Ohio: Arthur H. Clark Company, 1928.

Harris, Neil. *Humbug: The Art of P. T. Barnum*. Boston: Little, Brown and Company, 1973.

Havighurst, Walter. *Annie Oakley of the Wild West*. New York: MacMillan Co., 1954.

Heitman, Francis B. *Historical Register and Dictionary of the United States Army*. Washington, D.C.: Government Printing Office, 1903.

Hofstadter, Richard. *The Age of Reform*. New York: Vintage Books, 1960.

Hutton, Paul. "From Little Bighorn to Little Big Man: The Changing Image of a Western Hero in Popular Culture." *The Western Historical Quarterly* 7 (January 1976).

Ingraham, Col. Prentiss. *Buffalo Bill the Border King*. New York: Street and Smith, 1907.

Johannsen, Albert. *The House of Beadle and Adams and Its Dime and Nickel Novels*. Vols. 1, 2. Norman: University of Oklahoma Press, 1950.

Kasper, Shirl. *Annie Oakley*. Norman: University of Oklahoma Press, 1992.

King, James T. *War Eagle: The Life of General Eugene Carr*. Lincoln: University of Nebraska Press, 1963.

Kuykendall, Judge W. L. *Frontier Days*. Cheyenne, Wyo.: J. M. and H. L. Kuykendall Publishers, 1917.

Lavender, David. *Fort Laramie and the Changing Frontier*. Washington, D.C.: National Park Service, n.d.

Leonard, Elizabeth Jane, and Julia Cody Goodman. *Buffalo Bill: King of the Old West*. New York: Library Publishers, 1955.

Lindsay, Charles, ed. "The Diary of Dr. Thomas G. Maghee." *Nebraska History* 13 (July 1925).

Majors, Alexander. *Seventy Years on the Frontier*. Chicago: Rand, McNally & Company, 1893.

May, Henry F. *The End of American Innocence*. New York: Alfred A. Knopf, 1959.

Mitterling, Philip I. "Buffalo Bill and Carry Nation: Symbols of an Age." *North Dakota Quarterly* 50 (Winter 1982): 62–67.

Nieuwenhuyse, Craig Francis. *Six-guns on the Stage*. Ann Arbor, Mich.: University Microfilms International, 1984.

North, Luther. *A Man of the Plains: Recollections of Luther North*. Lincoln: University of Nebraska Press, 1961.

Nye, Russell. *The Unembarrassed Muse: The Popular Arts in America*. New York: Dial Press, 1970.

Patrick, Lucille Nichols. *The Best Little Town by a Dam Site or Cody's First 20 Years*. Cheyenne, Wyo.: Flintlock Publishing Co., 1968.

Peffer, William A. *Populism: Its Rise and Fall*. Lawrence: University Press of Kansas, 1992.

Peiss, Kathy. *Cheap Amusements*. Philadelphia: Temple University Press, 1986.

Powell, David Franklin. *Old Grizzley Adams, The Bear Tamer; or "The Monarch of the Mountains."* New York: M. J. Ivers & Co., 1899.

___. *The Dragoon Detective; or A Man of Destiny*. New York: Beadle & Adams, 1893.

Reddin, Paul L. "Wild West Show: A Study in the Development of Western Romanticism." Diss., University of Missouri, 1970.

Riis, Jacob A. *How the Other Half Lives*. New York: Dover Publications, 1971.

Riley, Paul D. "Red Willow Country Letters of Royal Buck, 1872–1873." *Nebraska History* 47 (December 1966).

___. "The Battle of Masscare Canyon." *Nebraska History* 54.

___. "Dr. David Franklin Powell and Fort McPherson." *Nebraska History* 51.

Roark, James L. *Masters without Slaves*. New York: W. W. Norton & Company, 1977.

Rollinson, John K. *Pony Trails in Wyoming*. Lincoln: University of Nebraska Press, reprint 1988.

Rosa, Joseph G. *They Called Him Wild Bill*. Norman: University of Oklahoma Press, 1964.

Russell, Don. *The Lives and Legends of Buffalo Bill*. Norman: University of Oklahoma Press, 1960.

___. *The Wild West*. Fort Worth, Tex.: Amon Carter Museum of Western Arts, 1970.

Russell, Don, ed. "Julia Cody Goodman's Memoirs of Buffalo Bill." *Kansas Historical Quarterly* 28, no. 4 (Winter 1962).

Sandoz, Mari. *The Buffalo Hunters*. New York: Hastings House, 1954.

Sayers, Isabelle S. *Annie Oakley and Buffalo Bill's Wild West*. New York: Dover Publications, 1981.

Schnapper, Morris Bartel. *American Labor: A Pictoral History*. Washington, D.C.: Public Affairs Press, 1972.

Sell, Henry Blackman, and Victor Weybright. *Buffalo Bill and the Wild West*. New York: Signet Key Books, 1959.

Siegel, Mark. *American Culture and the Classic Western Movie*. Japan: Eihosha, L.T.D., 1984.

Slotkin, Richard. "The Wild West." In *Buffalo Bill and the Wild West*. New York: Brooklyn Museum, 1981.

Smith, Henry Nash. *Virgin Land*. Cambridge, Mass.: Harvard University Press, 1950.

Sorg, Eric V. "The Skinning of White Beaver Powell." In *Old West*. Stillwater, Okla.: Western Publications, 1993.

Steckmesser, Kent Ladd. *The Western Hero in History and Legend*. Norman: University of Oklahoma Press, 1965.

___. *Western Outlaws: The "Good Badman."* Claremont, Calif.: Regina Books, 1983.

Swartout, Annie Fern. *Missie: The Life and Times of Annie Oakley*. Blanchester, Ohio: Brown Publishing Co., 1947.

Turner, Frederick Jackson. *The Frontier in American History*. New York: Henry Holt and Company, 1920.

Utley, Robert M. *Frontier Regulars*. Lincoln: University of Nebraska Press, 1973.

___. *The Lance and the Shield: The Life and Times of Sitting Bull*. New York: Ballantine Books, 1993.

Vaughn, J. W. *With Crook at the Rosebud*. Harrisburg, Pa.: Stackpole Co., 1956.

Vestal, Stanley. *Sitting Bull: Champion of the Sioux*. Norman: University of Oklahoma Press, 1957.

___. *Warpath*. Lincoln: University of Nebraska Press, 1984.

Walsh, Richard J. *The Making of Buffalo Bill: A Study in Heroics*. Indianapolis, Ind.: Bobbs-Merrill Company, 1928.

Walsh, Richard J., and Milton S. Salsbury. *The Making of Buffalo Bill*. Kissimmee, Fla.: Cody Publications, 1978.

Welch, Charles A. *History of the Big Horn Basin*. Salt Lake City, Utah: Deseret News Press, 1940.

Wetmore, Helen Cody. *Last of the Great Scouts: The Life Story of Col. William F. Cody as Told by His Sister*. Chicago: Duluth Press Publishing Company, 1899.

Wiebe, Robert H. *The Search for Order 1877–1920*. New York: Hill and Wang, 1967.

Wilstach, Frank J. *The Plainsman—Wild Bill Hickok*. Garden City, N.Y.: Sun Dial Press, 1937.

Winget, Dan. *Anecdotes of "Buffalo Bill" That Have Never Appeared in Print*. Chicago: Historical Publishing Company, 1927.

Wood, Elizabeth Lambert. "Arizona Hoof Trails." *Oracle Historian* (Summer 1980).

Yost, Nellie Snyder. *Buffalo Bill*. Chicago: The Swallow Press, 1979.

Newspapers

Illinois
Inter-Ocean (Chicago: 1881–1885).

Minnesota
Duluth Press serial story, Du Belyew, Encie. *The Silver Star; or Buffalo Bill's Beacon* (Duluth: Duluth Press, 30 September 1893 weekly to 24 March 1894).

Nebraska
Bee (Omaha: 1867–1872, 1901, 1906).
Daily Herald (Omaha: 1867–1872).

Wisconsin
Morning Chronicle (La Crosse: 1880–1906).
Republican and Leader (La Crosse: 1800–1906).

Archives and Libraries

American Heritage Center, Laramie, Wyoming

Bieneke Library, Yale University, New Haven, Connecticut

Buffalo Bill Historical Center, Cody, Wyoming

Carbon County Clerk's Office, Rawlins, Wyoming

Circus World Museum, Baraboo, Wisconsin

Denver Public Library, Denver, Colorado

Fillmore County Clerk's Office, Preston, Minnesota

Grand Encampment Museum, Encampment, Wyoming

Kansas State Historical Society, Topeka, Kansas

La Crosse County Clerk's Office, La Crosse, Wisconsin

La Crosse Historical Society, La Crosse, Wisconsin

Lanesboro Historical Society, Lanesboro, Minnesota

Library of Congress, Washington, D.C.

Murphy Special Collections, University of Wisconsin, La Crosse, Wisconsin

National Anthropological Archives, Washington, D.C.

National Archives, Washington, D.C.

National Museum of American History, Washington, D.C.

Nebraska State Historical Society, Lincoln, Nebraska

Omaha Historical Society, Omaha, Nebraska

Park County Historical Society, Cody, Wyoming

Scout's Rest Museum, North Platte, Nebraska

University of Louisville, Louisville, Kentucky

Wisconsin State Historical Society, Madison, Wisconsin

Wyoming State Archives, Cheyenne, Wyoming

Books of related interest from Ancient City Press

Mystic Healers and Medicine Shows
by Gene Fowler

When Six Guns Ruled: Outlaw Tales of the Southwest
by Marc Simmons

Following the Santa Fe Trail: A guide for Modern Travelers
by Marc Simmons

They "Knew" Billy the Kid:
Interviews with Old-Time New Mexicans
edited by Robert F. Kadlec

Ranchers, Ramblers, and Renegades:
True Tales of Territorial New Mexico
by Marc Simmons

Mean as Hell:
The Life of a New Mexico Lawman
by Dee Harkey

Along the Rio Grande:
Cowboy Jack Thorp's New Mexico
edited by Peter White and Mary Ann White